How to Speak Effectively:
Influence, Engage, & Charm

By Patrick King
Social Interaction and Conversation Coach at
www.PatrickKingConsulting.com

Table of Contents

CHAPTER 1: COMMUNICATION FUNDAMENTALS — 7

- THE LADDER OF INFERENCE — 7
- FRAMING — 20
- CHUNKING: ADJUSTING THE ZOOM BUTTON — 29
- THINK BEFORE YOU SPEAK — 41

CHAPTER 2: MASTERING STYLE AND TONE — 55

- ELIMINATE CRUTCH WORDS AND EMPTY LANGUAGE — 55
- UPSPEAK AND THE MYSTERY OF TONE — 65
- HOW TO USE SIGNPOSTS — 76

CHAPTER 3: PAINTING WITH WORDS — 89

- THE ART OF VIVID LANGUAGE: USE IMAGERY AND RHYTHM — 89
- HOW TO BE A MASTERFUL STORYTELLER — 100

CHAPTER 4: COMMUNICATION'S MOST UNDERRATED SKILL — 111

- ASKING THE RIGHT QUESTIONS — 111
- HOW TO BE A TRULY EFFECTIVE LISTENER — 124
- DON'T BE A CONVERSATIONAL NARCISSIST! — 135

CHAPTER 5: WHEN IT ALL GOES WRONG… — 145

- EFFECTIVE CONFLICT RESOLUTION — 145
- HOW TO MASTER HIGH-STAKES DISCUSSIONS AND STABILIZE INTENSE EMOTIONS — 157
- ASSERTIVE COMMUNICATION — 167
- GIVE AND TAKE: THE ART OF FEEDBACK — 181

SUMMARY GUIDE — 193

Chapter 1: Communication Fundamentals

The Ladder of Inference

In the chapter that follows, we're going to look closely at exactly what makes communication effective . . . and what makes it *mis*communication. We'll consider the importance of understanding the other person's frame of reference, how to frame your own position, what "chunking" is and how to use it, and how to adjust your mindset so you become a conscious, clean communicator.

But first, what is miscommunication? Have you ever been speaking with someone, feeling as though you are "reaching them," when all of a sudden, they say something that lets you know that you are both on completely different wavelengths? It can be a disorienting and frustrating experience, but miscommunication happens for a reason—and it can be avoided.

Poor communication arises as a result of a mismatch of perspectives, approach, or conversational skill.

Being an effective communicator means appreciating that the complicated process of communication doesn't happen by accident. **To avoid misunderstandings you need to consciously and actively take charge of the process**—and this is especially true when your message is subtle, nuanced, or very abstract.

If you examine any moment of miscommunication clearly, you'll see that understanding breaks down for a few reasons:

- One or both of you has failed to understand how the other is viewing things
- Faulty assumptions have been made, or someone has jumped to conclusions

In 1974, business professor Chris Argyris created a handy tool for better communication, which he called "the ladder of inference" (sometimes called "the ladder of inquiry"). The ladder is a metaphor for the way people think whenever they are given new information. It's about how new data and information is processed. What's useful about his metaphor is that it reminds us in a simple way that **different people tend to process information in different ways.** If we are unaware that this is happening, we can talk at cross-purposes—and miscommunication arises.

Before we look at the ladder, let's consider an example. Imagine a couple working together on a household budget. Jamie is looking back at the past six months and trying to find out where they overspent and why. Alex is looking ahead to the next six months and trying to figure out what kind of summer vacation they can afford.

They end up having an enormous argument, with Jamie thinking that Alex is not taking money concerns seriously, or taking responsibility for overspending, whereas Alex cannot see why Jamie is stuck on what is in the past and cannot be changed. They both find themselves saying "I'm just trying to get a handle on our financial situation!" and yet mysteriously they also both feel that the other one is getting in the way.

What's happened here?

According to Argyris, communication has broken down, and it's because Jamie and Alex are on different rungs of the ladder of inference. If you've ever experienced a communication breakdown of this kind, you'll know that it can be very subtle and hard to pinpoint. Often, we are only actually aware of our assumptions, expectations, and frames of reference *when they conflict with someone else's*!

But this is where the ladder comes in. It looks as follows. Imagine a ladder with each rung getting gradually smaller **from bottom to top**:

ACTIONS

BELIEFS

CONCLUSIONS

ASSUMPTIONS

MEANINGS

SELECTED DATA

OBSERVATIONS

Now imagine that this ladder is standing in a big puddle of water, which we'll call the POOL OF OBSERVATIONS. This pool contains all the possible observations we can make about the world—theoretically, there are infinite possibilities. The next rung up is OBSERVATIONS. These are all the observations that you select from the candidates of potential. We'll look at what causes you to select some observations and not others in just a moment.

The next rung is about the pieces of information you further select from these selected observations, SELECTED DATA—i.e., it's a subset. You're further narrowing down the data you are focusing on. The next rung is MEANING, which is the significance you attach to these selected observations. The next rung, ASSUMPTIONS, is what you do with this meaning. You extrapolate or make assumptions based on the meaning you've extracted from the observations.

On the next rung you come to CONCLUSIONS to make sense about what this all amounts to, and finally, these conclusions inform your BELIEFS about the world and your place in it. Consequently, every ACTION you take, the last rung, is informed by this long chain of inferences and meaning making. Furthermore, the ladder doesn't just go one way. Once you make meaning and take an action in accordance with those beliefs, then those beliefs actually tend to affect the data you are likely to select next time round on the SELECTED DATA rung.

Can you see where this is going? There are two potential problems:

1. Though everyone may begin in the same puddle of potential observations, each person ends up constructing *their own unique ladder* from those observations all the way up to the actions they take. If those ladders lead to completely different assumptions, meanings, beliefs, and ultimately actions, then conflict can arise.
2. Conflict can also occur, as we saw with Jamie and Alex, when two people are on different rungs and trying to talk with one another from different positions.

In our example, Jamie is on the SELECTED DATA and MEANING rungs, trying to understand what went wrong and piece it all together (and, honestly, assign blame . . .). Alex, however, is on the BELIEFS or ACTIONS rung, and is already looking for ways to move on from the fact that they overspent.

It may be, however, that even if Jamie and Alex were on the same rung, they may disagree on what meanings to ascribe to observations, and what beliefs and actions to take as a result. **However, good communication doesn't necessarily mean agreement—it means understanding.** Jamie and Alex can have a fruitful, productive conversation even though they ultimately disagree. At the same time, they can have an argument even when they both want the same thing and essentially agree!

How to Use the Ladder in Your Own Life

The ladder is an excellent way to identify, defuse, and resolve conflict. It's a way to shed light on misunderstandings and get everyone moving forward again. If you find yourself in a situation where you or others are "talking past one another," then this is your signal that communication is going to break down—or already has.

The first thing to do is check which rung each speaker is on. If the person you're talking to has an objection that comes from a rung lower than yours, it needs to be addressed first before moving on. Your discussion should focus on bringing you both up the ladder *together*. For example, if Alex identifies that Jamie is on a lower rung, then the objections made start to make more sense. Alex can now address them.

Jamie: "You're not listening. We spent five hundred dollars more last month on eating out than we said we would. That's a big deal!"

Alex: "Okay, it seems like you're really worried about how much we overspent. I agree with you, it's a lot. Why do you think it happened?" (Here, Alex is asking Jamie to move to the next rung, MEANING.)

Jamie: "Well, we were careless, that's all. We weren't paying attention."

Alex: "I agree. It crept up on us. Now I'm sure you'll agree with me, though, that there's nothing we can do about it now. And if we want to do better next time round, we need to start looking at the future." (Now, to the next rung—can you see the two ASSUMPTIONS made?)

Jamie: "Yes, okay. Let's do that."

Alex: "Unless we make some changes, we're going to be in big trouble (CONCLUSIONS). Now I know money's tight, but I still believe that going on vacations is very important, and I don't want to suddenly stop doing everything we enjoy (BELIEFS). So I think moving forward, I want to figure out some smart ways we can still do the things we love without spending too much money (ACTIONS)."

Jamie: "Yes, that makes a lot of sense. I want to do that too."

Now, there is no more disagreement in which Jamie keeps reiterating how bad they were to overspend, while Alex feels guilty for planning vacations. They're communicating again. Granted, in this example, we've kept things very simple and straightforward; in real life, each of these "rungs" may take a long time, perhaps even days. And though in our example Alex very neatly "leads" Jamie, in reality this process would be a lot more subtle, complex, and collaborative. There may well be disagreement or compromise. But ultimately communication is improved because people are reasoning together, rather than at cross-purposes.

The ladder can also be useful any time you are trying to get someone to understand

your own actions, or proposed actions. Whenever you want to "bring someone around" to your point of view, don't start with the top of the ladder—bring them along with you and take each step of the ladder at a time so they can see how the inferences and assumptions of your argument gradually build on one another. It's true that someone understanding your thought process doesn't necessarily have to agree with you afterward. The good thing is that if you use the ladder technique, you will almost always avoid misunderstandings and miscommunication, and you will give yourself the best chance of actually being heard.

Another great thing about the ladder is that it shows you that the process of thinking contains many separate, *sequential* components—and skipping one can sometimes lead to sloppy thinking and, of course, miscommunication. It can be useful sometimes to use the ladder to slow down and examine your own thought processes.

Try working backward almost "forensically":

1. What beliefs have inspired your actions?
2. What conclusions do you have about a situation, yourself, others, or the world that informed those beliefs?

3. What assumptions are you making? (A great question is to ask whether you really have much evidence for them, and investigate what changes if you make different assumptions or none at all).
4. What meaning are you ascribing to your experiences?
5. What are you focusing on? What data are you selecting from your environment to act on—or else, what information have you discounted, ignored, or forgotten about?
6. Finally, can you look once more with fresh eyes at the observations around you? For a moment, can you do this without any interpretation?

Asking these questions can reveal interesting ways that our own thinking has gone astray, and if we can get a better understanding of that, we instantly become better communicators. After all, how can we expect clear and conscious communication with others when we ourselves are unclear on our motivations, expectations, and the meaning we ascribe to any situation?

The ladder can be used formally or informally, and for big complex chunks of data as well as more simple information. It is highly adjustable, but its strength is that it forces you to look at things you might have taken for granted. For example, you might use the framework in a meeting you are leading. If you understand the meeting as an exercise in getting everyone to "think together," then you can structure the meeting so that it moves deliberately from one rung to the other. This gives you time to iron out objections or confusions rather than rushing ahead to the higher rungs and risking a full-on conflict.

A few further key insights as you use the ladder in your own communication:

Nobody is "wrong." The ladder is not there to help you find out who is to blame! Also, the person who is higher on the ladder isn't necessarily faster, more intelligent, more correct, or more motivated. As we've seen, misunderstandings usually arise because of *mismatch*—that doesn't mean that there has to be a good guy and a bad guy. It just means something is not aligning.

Switch focus from content to process. Too many arguments are sustained because people are distracted by the content of what is being said—but usually the problem is the *way* it's being said, and the reasoning behind that. As you talk to someone, become tuned in to the way they are thinking—and the way you are thinking!

Keep your ego out of it. Disagreement and conflict have a way of activating our defenses and making us wrongly believe that we are the model of good reasoning, and everyone else is mistaken, stupid, crazy, wrong, bad, etc. But slow down and consider your reasoning, their reasoning, and the way the two are interacting. Remember that you are not just applying the ladder analysis to them, but to yourself as well. You might feel like you want to stand on the top of your own ladder and yell your opinion to all who will hear it, but this is just ego talking and will get you nowhere.

Ask questions. Finally, one way to become a better communicator is to actively engage them in the process of examining the underlying reasoning behind action and opinion. Ask with genuine curiosity. Why do they think XYZ? What facts do they know, and what do those facts mean to them? Why? How?

To conclude, most of us experience the objective world subjectively and selectively. We focus on specific facts only, interpret what those facts mean based on certain assumptions, come to conclusions based on these assumptions, allow these conclusions to shape our beliefs, and then let these beliefs guide our action . . . as well as determine what facts we focus on in the future. This process can be an opportunity to create a strong, effective, and healthy way of looking at the world, or it can become an unconscious echo chamber that ends up amplifying and replicating the same errors again and again.

Framing

If you're like most people, you listen to respond. You're reactive. You let conversations go whichever way they go.

But good communicators approach things a little differently. They are more likely to proactively set the frame for a conversation. **What is a "frame"? It's simply the way you position your line of thinking by your particular choice of words and expression.** It's the kind of thing that will appear to be everywhere once you know to look for it. It's how we develop our arguments, "lead" our listeners along paths of reasoning and inference, and deliberately use language for a special purpose we have chosen.

Consider the following speech made by Barack Obama at the 2004 Democratic National Convention:

> *"There's not a liberal America and a conservative America; there's the United States of America. There's not a Black America and white America and Latino America and Asian America; there's the United States of America ...*
>
> *We are one people, all of us pledging allegiance to the stars and stripes, all of us defending the United States of America. In the end, that's what this election is about. Do we participate in a politics of cynicism, or do we participate in a politics of hope?"*

Notice how he has structured his speech—notice the frame by which he is delivering his message. He did not simply stand up on the stage and announce: "It's important for us to remember who we are as Americans" or even "it's time there was an African American president, and I'll give you some reasons why." Rather, he took seventeen long minutes to lead the audience to this conclusion themselves. Note in the above that he asks a rhetorical question, to which the only answer can be "we participate in a politics of hope." Notice the rhythm and repetition in the way he lays out the artificial differences between different types of Americans, then leads to his conclusion: "we are one people."

Obama (and indeed anyone delivering a persuasive speech of this kind) succeeds not because he effectively shows people what he thinks, but because he constructs a compelling frame in which to communicate that message. His listeners, then, go a step further from understanding and are stirred up enough to be inspired by him and agree with what he says.

When the frame of a conversation changes, everything changes. Everything takes on a different meaning. Therefore, it's simply not something we can leave to chance. Obama, of course, would have had this speech carefully written by experts, and he may well have rehearsed it for hours. Obama was known as a powerful and persuasive speaker, and it's in big part due to his understanding of how to frame himself and his message.

George Lakoff is an author and professor of cognitive science and linguistics. In his book *Don't Think of an Elephant!*, he explains how talking to people's frames is a powerful way of having them really hear you, saying that we mistakenly think that,

> *"if we just tell people the facts, since people are basically rational beings, they'll all reach the right conclusions. But we know from cognitive science that people do not think like that. People*

think in frames . . . to be accepted, the truth must fit people's frames. If the facts do not fit a frame, the frame stays and the facts bounce off.

Why?

Neuroscience tells us that each of the concepts we have—the long-term concepts that structure how we think—is instituted in the synapses of our brains. Concepts are not things that can be changed just by someone telling us a fact. We may be presented with facts, but for us to make sense of them, they have to fit what is already in the synapses of the brain. Otherwise, facts go in and then they go right back out. They are not heard, or they are not accepted as facts, or they mystify us: "Why would anyone have said that?" Then we label the fact as irrational, crazy, or stupid."

So, **a frame is the way we work with pre-existing concepts to ensure that the message we're sharing has the highest chance of being received**. Interestingly, it's also why Lakoff recommends resisting the frame of someone you're pushing against by refusing to use their language. This is because it is language that builds the frame—and if someone is not working in your interests, then the frame they choose will not be the frame you want.

In Obama's case, framing is used to persuade. But frames can have other uses and are especially helpful in navigating difficult, uncomfortable, or emotionally charged conflicts. Maybe the other person just refuses to listen or believe you. Maybe you both keep saying the same things over and over, and it's escalating. What's the solution? According to Lakoff, you both need to find a way to *get into the same frame.*

As a good communicator, it's your job to find out what story you could tell that will resonate with the other person. Remember—it's not about facts. It's about all the many different ways to look at those facts, and what that means for two people who find themselves in a conversation about them. Here are a few things to keep in mind:

1. Make sure that, as far as possible, you begin every conversation with a good idea of where you want it to go. Be proactive.
2. What is your frame? Your source of truth? The framework you're embedded in?

Really own this—it will help you find the metaphors and stories that will help you express your position.
3. Get the other person to see into this frame of yours by asking them questions. You want them to agree. Be careful and avoid using their story or their words.
4. Deliberately engineer the structure of your story so that it leads toward the kind of solutions you want. It's about focus.

Reading the above, you may think that setting a conversational frame may be a little manipulative. Isn't thinking in this way precisely the thing that leads to stubborn standoffs in conversations? Well, yes and no. **The truth is, we are all using frames all the time.** It's just a question of whether we're consciously aware of it, how those frames work, to what end, and in service of whom and what. Being a good communicator means understanding all this and proactively taking charge. This is more often than not a win-win scenario.

Let's look at an example. Imagine a potential client is interested but has concerns about the price you're charging. What you don't want to do in this case is bombard them with facts (you might call them "reasons") to change their mind. It won't work. What you need to do is consider the best frame for the case you want to make. And to do that, you need to understand the frame they're already in, the nature of their objections and fears, and what exactly it is you're asking them to do.

This might allow you to realize that the person is hesitant because they are unsure of the real value of what you're offering. They are very, very tired of being aggressively marketed to and just want something that works. So you say that they're right—it is expensive. There are people who don't buy because it's not in their budget, and that's okay. But you do have many satisfied clients who, having taken the leap, are now really glad they did—and you'd be happy to put them in touch. Otherwise, you totally respect their decision either way, and they know where to find you if they change their mind.

Can you feel the frame? Can you see how this response actually pulls the potential client into that frame with you? There is nothing in it for the person to push against—and a lot to agree with. As Dwight D. Eisenhower said, "Motivation is the art of getting people to do what you want them to do because they want to do it." In this example, you are using a frame that gives you the best chance of actually reaching this prospective client and getting them to behave in the way you want them to behave.

In the same way, a frame can change anything. It can turn a restriction and a limit into "safety" and "comfort." It can position a loss as a gain or a gain as a loss. It can appoint an adversary as a teacher, and a friend as a saboteur. The luxury fashion brand Hermes sells a handbag, the "Birkin." But not just anyone can buy the handbag; there are only a limited number available, and you have to be invited to spend the roughly fifty thousand dollars to have one. The company will only sell to those they consider worthy, and in fact don't even fully advertise their selection criteria, and do not display the bag in ordinary stores. Their tactics around this item are kept under a deliberate veil of mystery.

Hermes has completely inverted the conventional buyer-seller frame and created their own: In this frame, instead of the company marketing themselves so they are selected by the consumer, the consumer fights to be considered a potential buyer and feels privileged to cough up the fifty thousand dollars.

Every person you ever communicate with will have a lifetime of experiences behind them, and these have taught them in gradual increments to adopt certain beliefs and worldviews (hopefully not too many as bizarre as Hermes'). Many of these views will be unconscious. But that doesn't stop them from being strongly influenced by these beliefs, which seep through and infiltrate everything they do and say, as well as everything they're able to hear or agree with.

Think again about Obama's speech. There would have been many different people in the crowd that night, and a lot of them will have possessed viewpoints and frames that *didn't* match the one Obama was presenting. For example, many Democrats who are politically involved enough to attend conventions and rallies *do* tend to think that there is such a thing as a "liberal America and a conservative America, a Black America and white America"—after all, they were there to show support for the democrats, not the conservatives, and specifically for Obama himself precisely *because* he was a Black American, not because his race didn't matter.

This is the power of framing—it can so thoroughly change context, shift meanings, and create new understandings that it allows you to not only *have* a conversation but *steer* a conversation. This steering is so powerful that it can actually remake meaning entirely and cause people to completely change not just their opinions but the way they arrive at those opinions. Obama could have framed himself as a victim or as an angry avenger. He could have highlighted the frame of justice, or the frame of prosperity. He could, in essence, have chosen any frame in the world.

When someone uses their power to frame and influence in a good way, we call them leaders and are happy to be inspired by them. When their frames dominate and diminish us, we call them bullies and tyrants. Importantly—it's the same skill!

Reality is fixed . . . but the *meaning* of reality is dynamic and subject to change. It is not absolute but contextual, not passively received but actively constructed. This is where communication takes place, and where you have your greatest chance for making connections, being heard, and influencing others.

Chunking: Adjusting the Zoom Button

Take a look at this conversation:

A: Oh, wow, so you're a music teacher! How long have you been doing that?
B: Oh, about ten years now, at least.
A: Cool. And that whole time you taught the French horn?
B: Well, no. That's my main instrument, but I do oboe as well.
A: Huh. I've heard that the French horn is really difficult.
B: Yeah, it can be. A lot of my students end up quitting, sorry to say!
A: Oh, yeah? How long do they stay before they usually quit?
B: How long? Uh . . . I'm not sure. Everyone's different, I guess. I'd say the ones who leave do so pretty quickly. But that could be for all sorts of reasons. It's complicated, I think. But you know early on whether you love the instrument or not.
A: Oh, totally. So maybe, like, they'd quit after the first lesson?
B: Uh . . . no, not always. Sometimes a month? I don't know.
A: Do they ever tell you before they go or do they just disappear?

And on and on. What's your feeling about this conversation? Reading it again, can you spot the point at which is starts to kind of grind along? You can almost feel the moment where B starts to get bored. Why?

Before we consider the answer, let's look at another example:

A: Oh, wow, so you're a music teacher! How long have you been doing that?
B: Oh, about ten years now, at least.
A: Cool. That's a long time. Do you think you'll always teach?
B: Well, I do sometimes wonder. It's rewarding, but . . . people's attitudes to learning have changed so much over the years, you know?
A: I can imagine. People seem to just have less and less patience these days. What do you think's causing it?
B: Well, who knows. Take your pick, right? I mean, I have some very good students, so I can't complain.
A: Oh, I'm sure. Do you think that overall your students' motivations are changing over time?
B: Hm, could be. It's hard to say.
A: Do you think that you've had to adapt the way you teach them to accommodate for how different students are today compared with ten years ago? I often feel like we focus too much on technique in this country, and so little on the art side. Do you find that?

Now consider what you think of this conversation. It's completely different, but somehow something is still not quite working. The big problem with both conversations (other than A asking a barrage of questions and B being somewhat unresponsive) is a question of *chunking*.

In neuro-linguistic programming, the word "chunking" is used to describe the way in which we can group pieces of information. We can chunk "up" or "down:"

Chunking up means to ask questions or make comments in such a way as to combine information and make it more abstract and more general. It's the process of looking for things that are coming, or "zooming out" to see the overarching theme, pattern, or structure that simplifies all the smaller details you're looking at. So someone gives you a long list of all the pets they've had throughout their life, and you chunk up by saying, "So you're a real animal lover, huh?"

Chunking down goes the other way. It's when we ask questions or make comments that move the conversation from the general and abstract to the more specific. Someone says they love animals, and you ask them, "Do you have a pet?" In doing so, you're asking for a more *specific* instance of the general claim they've just made, i.e., zooming in.

Basically, chunking is a way to turn the dial on the level of detail occurring in a conversation. Let's return to our examples above. In the first example, Speaker A asks questions that lead to them zooming in on the idea of students quitting and exactly when they quit and why. It's as though each question drills deeper and deeper into this one chosen thread—perhaps to the boredom of Speaker B!

The second conversation has a different problem. Here, Speaker A keeps asking questions that open up the conversation to a more abstract level. But in time, these questions just seem to go nowhere. They are soon talking about students in general, and then all people and their total lack of patience, and then the entire system of music education in the whole country—there's a load of sweeping generalization and broad abstraction. Again Speaker B is not quite enjoying this flight into the abstract!

Chunking up questions/phrases/themes can look like:

- What does that mean?
- Let's look at the big picture . . .

- How does that connect to . . . ?
- Why did all of that happen?
- What pattern is emerging?

Chunking down, on the other hand, could sound like:

- What happened next?
- Can you provide a specific detail? (For example, what was his name? How much did it cost?)
- Tell me more about . . .
- When did this happen, and in what order?

Which is better to use—chunking up or down? The answer is neither, because a good conversation contains a dynamic balance of both of them. We can zoom in and out to various levels of detail and abstraction according to our needs. (We'll explore this more in a later chapter when we look at "funnel questions.")

Start at a broad, general level and work your way down. This may correspond with more open-ended questions, but it doesn't necessarily have to:

1. Start with chunking up to define the "territory" of your conversation, state the

parameters of the problem, or gently introduce a new conversation or topic.
2. Gradually chunk down, but **do not ask more than three chunking down questions in a row.** Find out things like specific goals, motivations, problems, interpretations, examples, etc.
3. Then zoom out again with another chunking up question. Again, try not to ask more than three of these in a row.

The point of zooming in and out is to avoid either extreme: Get too abstract and lofty and you risk creating a stiff, impersonal, and vague conversation about nothing and everything. On the other hand, linger too long on chunking down questions and you can get lost, stuck, or distracted by irrelevant details.

A good metaphor is to imagine that you and your conversation partner are mutually navigating your way up a winding mountain path, using a map. Sometimes, you'll both want to lean in and engage with the finer details of exactly where you are—the rocks and trees and so on. You'll focus on this turn or that turn, and the one foot in front of the other. But every once in a while, you have to consult the map and get a bigger picture of what you're doing. You need to look up and take in the horizon, or glance behind you to see how far you've advanced up the mountain and how much longer you have to go. You might even take a break and consider the whole reason for climbing the mountain in the first place! In any case, good mountaineers have both skills—they pay attention to the gravel beneath their boots, but also look up and around them and engage in the broader task.

The ideal conversation, then, would be a comfortable mix of the first and second of our examples above. For instance, instead of continuing to dwell on the students who quit, and exactly when they quit and why, Speaker A could take a metaphorical step back, allow the conversation to breathe a little, and take the opportunity to chunk up. Similarly, three or four chunking up questions into the second conversation is a good time to stop talking abstractly and probe for some specifics.

Conversational Extremist: The Nitpicker

In our examples, chunking up or down is something we can locate in a single question or comment. But it can often be more subtle than this. **"Nitpickers" are people who have a longstanding tendency to have conversations constantly take place on a concrete, literal, and detailed level.** The result can be a conversational style that is felt by others to be very dull, dragging, and uninspired. It's like the conversation gets "stuck in the weeds" and never really launches.

This is the person who, when you tell them you've met the love of your life, will be curious about what time in the morning you met them and what their name is and whether you spell that name with one L or two.

We tend to become conversational nitpickers ourselves for a few reasons. We may be anxious and trying to control the course of the conversation but inadvertently keep it muzzled to endless mundane details. We may be bored ourselves. The way out is simple: If you find that you or your listener is getting bored or distracted, sit back (sometimes literally!) and ask an open-ended, completely abstract question. Say something about an intangible concept. Introduce a metaphor, or even a controversial and nuanced opinion. This should kick the conversation back into gear.

Conversational Extremist: The Philosopher

The other extreme is the person who never, ever comes down from some towering abstract conversational heights and seems to always be looking down at humans and all the petty details of their lives . . . a bit like a philosopher. These are the people who will constantly try to make isolate observations or single anecdotes mean something about a grander political, social, or philosophical narrative. You might want to rant a little about someone who was late, and they respond with a deep-and-meaningful deconstruction of the entire notion of lateness, of all mankind's tendencies to rebel against artificial segmentation of this imaginary construct called time, and to finish off, some complex psychoanalysis of the late person—not just this person in question, but all people who are late.

The conversational philosopher is someone who is always looking for theories, patterns, and overarching themes, but this can come across as pompous, cold, and irrelevant. The solution, here, is also obvious: Come back to earth with a question about *this* person's *specific* life in the here and now. This should immediately anchor and ground the conversation, with a side effect of making you seem more human, more approachable, and more relaxed.

Chunking up or down, then, is not just a cognitive exercise about how information is managed. It's also about the degree of openness or closedness in a conversation, the overall sense of flow, and the extent that either levity or seriousness is allowed to dominate.

Use chunking up questions when you want to summarize, contextualize, consolidate, or get some distance—theoretical or emotional. This is a focus on an overarching organization, on purpose and intention.

Use chunking down questions when you want to expand on some point, zoom in, confirm, or get to grips with the more "real" aspects of the conversation. This is a focus on how the overarching themes express themselves in specific ways, on unique experience, and on the details: who, where, when, how, what, and why.

Finally, **pay attention to chunking in conflict situations.** You may discover that at least part of the problem is that two people are talking with different chunking tendencies. For example, your boss may call you in with the intention of discussing an issue. Your boss keeps listing out all instances of this issue and expanding on the details of each. You get impatient because you are eager to understand what all of it means—what is the single insight or conclusion you are meant to come to? Your boss sees you wanting to boil everything down and find some common cause for each transgression, but assumes this means you are not accepting the fact that there are many offenses, not just one. You see your boss endlessly listing grievances but without synthesizing them into anything you can act on. And round and round you both talk, both unable to reach one another because you're operating at completely different levels of detail.

When communication has devolved to this extent, the way back to a shared frame of reference is to ask questions or make comments that *gradually* close the gap.

"What is that an example of?"
"Is there something that connects all these observations?"
"What one thing do you want me to take from this conversation?"

On the other hand, if you're having a conflict with someone who is being overly vague and abstract, try to help them zoom in by asking things like:

"Can you give me a specific example of what you're talking about?"

"When did this event happen? With whom? How?"
"Can you pinpoint the exact moment it all went wrong?"

Think Before You Speak

"I just call it like I see it."
"I'm being honest."
"That's not what I *meant* to say."
"I'm just being me."
"I don't do small talk."

Have you ever said any of the above? One major impediment to health, effective communication is a set of subtle but very damaging beliefs about what is actually required of us as humans when we speak to others. **Some of these beliefs come from the idea that as long as we are authentic, sincere, and share our emotions, that's enough; in other words, our intentions matter, and how we articulate ourselves is less important.**

Nothing could be further from the truth! Good communicators know that you cannot just, well, blurt out whatever enters your mind. You need to be deliberate. You need to consciously *filter* what you say. You need to speak with purpose and discipline. If you've ever said something you later regretted or really "put your foot in it," then this is a sign that you could use more deliberation in the way you communicate!

The first thing is to subtly challenge the idea that communication is solely about expressing yourself, your position, or your emotions. It is not really relevant whether you have a strong feeling about something, whether you feel like you're right (or even if you *are* right!), or whether you are overcome by this or that impulse in the moment. Since communication is a social activity, it involves others, and that automatically means that a portion of all communication is *simply not about you*. People who understand and work with this insight are ultimately better at communication than those who keep on stubbornly insisting "it's not my fault that they misunderstood me!"

Being a conscious and careful communicator means you avoid causing offense or misunderstanding, you boost your credibility and maturity in other peoples' eyes, and you generally keep yourself out of trouble! Speaking without thinking, however, often occurs because we're impatient, we're conversational narcissists (more on this later in the book), we are not good at listening, or simply we're excited and get carried away with sharing what we want to share.

Not everything you think and feel needs to be shared. Not everything that pops into your head needs to be expressed. To decide what qualifies an idea to be shared, ask yourself the following questions:

1. Do I have good motives?

Is what you're going to say helpful or useful to yourself or anyone else? Be honest about what your motives are. Many people butt in during conversations to share some tidbit of information that is completely irrelevant, simply because it satisfies their own ego to say something and impress others. Be real and assess whether what you're saying moves things forward and contributes to the shared goal of the conversation (i.e., not some hidden agenda of your own).

Some people will say something along the lines of "if you can't say something nice, don't say anything at all." But sometimes, you *will* have to express something that's not "nice," especially if you are defending a boundary or addressing conflict. Still, your motives should be to share any grievance or disagreement with the intention of clarifying and resolving it, rather than to blame and shame. This is why motive matters. You may be able to fool the other person that you are saying something out of concern or genuine misunderstanding, but at least be honest with yourself and check whether you're speaking for some other, less noble reason.

2. Is it true?

Opinions, perspectives, and desires are one thing. But ask if, beyond this, you are actually saying something you know to be a falsehood. This may seem an obvious point to labor, but often we insert little falsehoods into what we say without being conscious of it. We exaggerate, we minimize, we omit important information, or we present our best guess as more certain than it really is. Again, it ties into motive. Are we genuinely and honestly sharing what we know, or are we trying to come across as an expert?

In the realm of our own perceptions and experiences, of course, nothing is really "true" or "false"—it is our unique experience. But be careful that you never act as though something being true *for you* automatically makes it true for another person. Here, being truthful means owning and acknowledging your own perspective, while not overstepping and behaving as though that perspective were truth.

3. Am I breaking confidences?

It goes without saying: never share something you've been asked to keep private. Gossip is awful and degrades the speaker, the listener, and the person being talked about in equal measure, but you can still break confidences even without technically being in gossip territory. Ask yourself this question: If the person you're talking about was present, would they be okay with hearing what you're saying about them?

4. Is it considerate?

No, you don't always have to be *kind*. Some situations in life call for communication even when we don't like or approve of the person in front of us, or where "kindness" isn't really appropriate. But you do have to be civil, polite, and considerate. You do have to show the other person a degree of non-negotiable respect. Sometimes, what you want to say may be true, it may be necessary, and you may be well within your rights to say it—but that still doesn't entitle you to be rude about it. In this case, remember that etiquette and manners are not something you do merely for the other person's sake, but something you do to communicate a degree of respect for yourself.

An option is to use the THINK acronym—which stands for True, Helpful, Inspiring, Necessary, or Kind. As we've seen, you don't need to have all of these, but if what you want to say ticks only one or two boxes, you're probably better off keeping silent or rewording your message.

All of this can only be achieved when you do something essential: **stop and think**. **Get into the habit of pausing before you talk, or even just *mentally* pausing**. Even a few seconds of forethought can be enough (deep down, we usually know whether something is a good idea or not even without going through the above questions—we just need to slow down enough to realize that we know!). If you're not really sure, then err on the side of staying silent. It's always possible to speak up later; it's never possible to un-say what's already been said.

Understanding "Clean Communication"

Imagine that a woman says to her husband, "Can you please take out the trash?"

Now imagine that she instead says, "Can you please take out the trash for a change?"

You can probably see which one is "clean" communication, and which one is a little *dirty*. Saying "for a change" adds a hostile blaming element that is not part of the main message, but forms a secondary piece of communication. This charge may be added in consciously or unconsciously. On the other hand, clean, smooth communication conveys a message without adding in any kind of "negative charge."

Any time your communication is serving a double role of delivering extra shame, anger, ridicule, guilt-tripping, manipulation, lies, and so on, it's no longer clean. Imagine the husband hears the second phrase from above and responds, "Take it out yourself." The wife may then (rightly) see this as an attack and respond, "Why are you so mean to me? All I did was ask you nicely to take the trash out!" As you can imagine, a fight ensues, in part because the wife's initial communication was *unconsciously* unclean. That didn't stop her husband from responding to what she was really communicating!

Whether consciously unclean (arguably a bit easier to deal with) or unconsciously unclean, this type of communication is a kind of *anti*-communication. It creates misunderstandings, hurt feelings, and barriers. Have you ever had a conversation with someone who on the surface seemed to be saying and doing all the right things, but you still somehow felt bad afterward? Maybe you had a weird physical sensation in your gut, or you felt like something was amiss. It might have felt like you were being lied to, manipulated, or subtly insulted... chances are, you were the recipient of some unclean communication.

Let's take a look at another example. The wife says to the husband, "Can you please take the trash out?" The husband hears this and, in his mind, interprets it to mean something like, "You're a lazy good-for-nothing and I have to talk to you like a child!" He responds in the same way, "Take it out yourself!" As you can see, the misunderstanding is now on the part of the listener/receiver. Here, the husband is overly sensitive, and has allowed his own issues to distort the message he's receiving. Again, the communication is unclean.

Whether snags happen on side A or side B, and whether they are done consciously or unconsciously, they can degrade communication. Even worse, little snares and hiccups can compound over time, creating animus and a feeling of negativity that is hard to shift once it's underway. This "toxic residue" can lead to more intense conflict in time or even a big blow out, so it's best to keep on top of communication as it happens, practicing, if you will, a kind of routine "communication hygiene." This cleans up little misunderstandings and conflicts before they become big ones.

You'll know that there is some residue in your communication with someone when one or both of you feels:

A little wary, nervous, or uncomfortable
Any combativeness and defensiveness
Lies, deception, or lowered trust
General upset or high emotional intensity

Now, the "dirt" in communication can be accidental, or it can be deliberate. If it's accidental, the idea is to stop, take a step back, and address it. Many innocent mistakes turn not-so-innocent if not addressed in this way. "Hey, I just wanted to talk to you about something. You asked me earlier to take the trash out, and it felt like you were kind of implying that I don't pull my weight or something. I don't know if I've got that wrong; is that what you were trying to say?" Importantly, in addressing something, you need to work hard not to introduce more unclean language!

If, however, the unclean communication is intended, then the approach is to go in to conflict resolution. "Well, actually, if we're going to be honest about it, I have been feeling like I'm doing too much of the housework lately." The thing is, communication can be clean even during conflict. So long as messages are being shared *without* introducing extra negativity, then the conversation is clean and likely to be productive.

First make a promise to yourself that you will use clean language as often as you can. Make a commitment that you will be straightforward, honest, and respectful, and will never resort to underhandedness, passive aggression, or innuendo. This takes a degree of conscious maturity as well as discipline.

According to clean communication experts Matthew McKay, Patrick Fanning, and Kim Paleg, the ideal communication attitude is **"taking responsibility for the effect of what you say."** It also means owning the consequences of your speech, even, and maybe especially if, you're not quite conscious of what you're doing. Do your best to create a conversational space where you can work honestly and respectfully through any conflicts or disagreements. Leave out harmful speech, accusations, "barbed" language, and insinuations that might hurt and attack another person—and do it no matter how upset or wronged you feel. Follow the "ten commandments of clean language" to keep you on the straight and narrow and spare yourself and others a load of unnecessary drama:

1. **Don't use judgment words and loaded terms** ("pigsty" or "lazy").
2. **Don't use "global" labels**, i.e., make sweeping generalizations or use absolute statements ("you haven't taken out the trash in two weeks" rather than "you're an untidy person," which takes a swipe at the person's *entire being*, not just their behavior).
3. **Don't send "you" messages** of blame and accusation ("I'm stressed" is better than "you're stressing me").
4. **Stay away from old history**—stick to the issue at hand and let bygones go.
5. **Avoid negative comparisons** ("You're a slob just like my ex was").
6. **Never threaten, even subtly** ("If you can't be bothered to do the trash, it makes me wonder why I bother to do any of *my* chores"). Control and manipulation only create escalating defensiveness.

7. **Describe your feelings** rather than use them as a weapon or a "point" you've scored ("You've really gone and riled me up this morning! Why do you always insist on hurting me like this?").

8. **Keep your body language open, relaxed, and receptive**. Call off a difficult conversation until you're calmer, if necessary.

9. **Use whole messages**. Incomplete messages are more likely to be taken out of context. A whole message contains observations, thoughts, feelings, and needs/wants. For example, "I see the trash is piling up (observation), and I realize you haven't taken it out for a long time (thoughts). When I see that I have to do it, even though it's your chore, I feel overwhelmed and annoyed. I'd really like for you to keep up your end of the housework as we agreed (wants/needs)."

10. **Be clear.** If you have a question, ask. If you want something, request it. Avoid using passive language, innuendo, or hints ("Is there some special reason you've decided to let us all live in filth, or . . .?"). Be direct and clear.

Summary:

- Poor communication arises as a result of a mismatch of perspectives, approach, or conversational skill. People process

information differently, but to avoid misunderstandings, communicate consciously and use the "ladder of inference." It shows the unique way that people use their experiences to make meaning: observations > selected data > meanings > assumptions > conclusions > beliefs > actions.
- Conflict can occur when people are on different rungs. To improve communication, see where people are and how their ladder of inference is working for them, then speak to that, in sequence, and without blame or shame.
- Good communicators deliberately create their own frames during conversations and position their line of thinking by using specially chosen words, expressions, and images. Change frames and you change meaning.
- Deliberately engineer your conversational frame and invite the other person in using pre-existing concepts they're familiar with to improve the chances they'll be receptive. Remember that reality is fixed, but the *meaning* of reality is dynamic and subject to change.
- Chunking is about the way we group information. Chunking up is grouping

specific instances into a larger overall abstract pattern or theory, while chunking down makes inferences from the general to the specific. Keeping the level of detail varied and appropriate creates a better flowing conversation than one that relies too heavily on chunking up or chunking down.
- It is a mistake to think that authenticity, expression, and sincerity are enough—*how* we articulate ourselves matters. Consciously filter what you say: Is it true, kind, and helpful?
- Take responsibility for what you say and practice clean communication—i.e., without hidden negative meanings.

Chapter 2: Mastering Style and Tone

Eliminate Crutch Words and Empty Language

So, um, you probably already, like, know what crutch words are and, well, how they can undermine your communication and stuff, you know. Right? If that makes sense?

It's not uncommon to feel a little flustered when speaking. It's not uncommon to feel distracted, unprepared, or unfocused. After all, the communication we're talking about is everyday communication—not carefully crafted speeches and presentations. Natural speech is often a little disjointed, loose, and open-ended. Crutch words or "filler words" can act like necessary padding or pauses to help us catch our breath, collect our thoughts, and process the next thing we want to say.

The trouble is when this kind of fluff language takes over and starts detracting from the overall message. **A crutch word helps prop you up, but it can make you harder to understand, hurt your credibility, and distract from what you're saying.** So much of what we say is socially and culturally coded, and filler words can come with an enormous set of assumptions, insinuations, and prejudices.

Words like *um, ah, well, you know, like, so, right, okay*, and *hm* can be like little speed bumps that interrupt the flow of your message. It's easy to see why—if you're talking to someone who is showing you that every third or fourth word they use essentially has no meaning, are you likely to pay more or less attention to what they say? The irony is that in using crutch words to fill an awkward silence, we end up diluting our message and making it *less* likely that people pay attention to all those other, non-crutch words.

More than this, using crutch words can actively annoy people and signal a subtle lack of conversational awareness and etiquette. Consider that when you open your mouth, you are "taking the floor," even if it's in a very casual and free-form setting. You are holding the mic, so to speak. If people get the sense that you are hogging this position without really saying anything, they are likely to get annoyed or bored, and they may be tempted to interrupt or just ignore you.

Get Comfortable with Pausing

To get rid of an overreliance on crutch words, you need to learn to do one thing: embrace silence. Usually, filler words and fluff are there to deal with a mild sense of anxiety, to fill the void, and to keep up feeling of flow when you're not quite sure what you're saying next. But if you actively embrace those (natural) pauses in speech, you empower yourself to be a more proactive, conscious, and confident speaker. You are not afraid of awkward silences—you are actively using them as one of the many tools you have in your conversational itinerary.

If you have a bad crutch word habit, don't worry—this can actually be used to your advantage. By replacing every crutch word with a thoughtful, assured pause, you communicate a few powerful things to your audience:

You are confident, either in yourself or in what you have to say. You do not feel that you need to quickly say your piece or rush through what you're saying for fear that you'll be interrupted or ignored. In treating your own message with this kind of attention and respect, you convey to others a belief in its value, and they can't help but do the same.

You show consideration for your audience. If someone is blundering and blathering on with very little thought for how clear their message is or how it may be coming across, they signal a disregard for the other person. All of us need to carefully consider how we present ourselves, and too many filler words can make for a boring and confusing listening experience for an audience. However, if other people get the sense that you are being deliberate about how you speak, you create a frame of mutual respect and consideration, which automatically elevates whatever conversation you're having.

It helps you stay calm. A pause is a moment in which you can gather yourself—and it's also a moment for the audience to process and digest what you're sharing. It's the difference between gobbling down a meal without thinking versus savoring each bite and pausing after each mouthful. The breath is connected to our state of anxiety—and if we're talking *constantly*, we're usually not breathing, and this fuels anxiety. Just stop, take a breath, and let the conversation expand a little and relax.

Finally, a pause can actually help you make your point. It's a mistake to think that silence is empty space or some kind of lost opportunity where you could have been speaking instead. A pause has power. Pausing at the right moment can alert your audience to the fact that you're about to say something important. It can help you build suspense and then release it. When you pause after something important, it can show the audience that you want them to really think about what you've just said. It gives you time to lean on other, non-verbal elements of your communication—such as your eye contact or body language. This can be more effective that just talking and talking.

Here is a two-step exercise you can try to break the crutch word habit and come across with more confidence and clarity.

Step 1: Pay attention. Actually listen to how you currently speak. This requires awareness in the moment, but it's even better if you can somehow record yourself during a conversation so you can play it back and see just how often you're relying on crutch words. You may be surprised! Try to notice not only when you're resorting to filler and fluff, but also to how this is impacting the conversation, how people's energy and attention levels are changing, how the conversation is flowing, and how anxious or confident you feel. Recording may be difficult, but you can also gain some insight by filming yourself telling a story. The idea is to get a good snapshot of the role this kind of language is presently playing in your life.

Step 2: The next bit is difficult but becomes easier with practice. Just keep quiet! Force yourself to say nothing instead of using a crutch word. You don't have to speak in a smooth, uninterrupted flow—just stay quiet if you're not sure what to say. Try to teach yourself that a pause is not a problem. Sure, if you just go silent for longer than five or six seconds, your listeners may start to wonder, but you may discover you seldom need that long to gather your thoughts, and that people are rather tolerant and will wait.

Then, repeat step 1 and notice how different it feels to pause instead of um and ah. Notice how you feel and how other people respond to you. You may also find that pausing in this way has other related benefits: You speak more slowly, more deliberately, and with more assuredness. You find yourself taking yourself more seriously!

The Dangers of "Hedging Language"

Imagine someone said the following to you:

"I was just wondering, I don't know, maybe we could potentially slow down a little with this new launch, just until we have more clarity on the funding situation. I don't mean to offend or anything, don't get me wrong, and I suppose this could just be, like, my issue, but I just feel that we could possibly pause here and, uh, reassess. Do you know what I mean? Haha, sorry if all that doesn't make any sense!"

Do you get the feeling that this person is calm, confident, and self-assured? Do you get the feeling that they are knowledgeable, competent experts? Are you inspired to listen to them and come along to their point of view?

Probably not. "Hedging" or "softening" language is a way to reduce what we're saying, to make it smaller, more polite, and less certain. It absolutely has a place whenever tact, diplomacy, and etiquette are required. In fact, it plays a vital role in communication of all kinds. However, like filler words and crutches, it can do more harm than good.

Imagine the same message conveyed as follows:

"I think we're moving a little fast on this. I would prefer personally to slow down until we have more clarity on the funding situation, although I do appreciate this may not be the majority view. What's your take on it? Is it essential that we launch this week?"

The message is the same, but the frame has positioned the speaker in an entirely different light.

Watch out for the following:

Maybe, could be, might, possibly, potentially, etc. Using these words is often an attempt to convey the uncertainty of the information, but it only makes *you* look uncertain.
Instead, say: *What you mean. Be direct and assertive without being rude.*

Does that make sense? Sorry I'm not making sense. Don't deliberately invite people to devalue what you say. Usually, people say this not when they're afraid of being

misunderstood, but when they want to signal submission and compliance.
Instead, say: *Nothing. Say what you mean, and if the other person misunderstands, they can ask for clarification.*

Do you know what I mean? Right? Don't you agree? This can come across as excessively seeking approval or validation . . . and consequently communicating that you don't feel sure in what you're saying. This can put people on the spot or make you seem needy or unreliable.
Instead say: *"What's your opinion on this?"*

I feel, I suppose, it's just me, I wonder, I'm worried, etc. Using "I feel" when you really mean "I think" or even "I believe" weakens your position. Using lots of emotive, self-effacing, or self-referencing language can create a frame that makes you look reactive and passive.
Instead say: *"I think," or simply state your perceptions without personalizing or psychologizing them.*

Hedging language, as you've probably noticed, tends to happen more with women. Whether women are naturally more effusive and submissive in conversations, or social norms have conditioned women to diminish themselves when speaking up, is a moot point. Whatever the truth, sadly there *are* some asymmetries in the way people perceive male and female speakers. A woman, for example, may be perceived as bossy and domineering when behaving in ways that are considered merely assertive for men, yet if she uses hedging language, she will not really be taken seriously. In the same way, a man may be encouraged to present himself as more certain and in control than he really feels, causing misunderstandings. Yet if he uses softer, more hedging language, again he will be perceived as *less* trustworthy and competent, even when this really signals a more nuanced and sophisticated understanding of his own message.

All of this is to say that something like hedging or crutch words are not *absolute* phenomena, but rather something that interacts with culture, gender, and so on. Furthermore, you may consciously choose to use hedging if you actually want to come across as non-threatening (for example, in diffusing conflict or in a tricky negotiation).

When speaking (especially in a professional context), it's almost always better to be

- concise

- calm
- clear

This **does not** mean rude or curt.

Upspeak and the Mystery of Tone

A related linguistic phenomenon is what is called upspeak (also called uptalk, "valley girl speak," or high rising terminal—HRT). Even if you've never heard the name of this phenomenon, you already know what it is, and you've heard plenty of it whether you know it or not!

Upspeak is when the last word of a declarative sentence (i.e., a statement) is said with a rising pitch, the same way a question does.

In 1993, journalist James Gorman wrote an article for *The New York Times* where he put a name to this phenomenon. It's not just a linguistic phenomenon but a complex stereotype that focused on upper-middle class young women who lived in the Southern California valleys. This way of speaking became wildly popular and emulated by many, but it also came to be vilified culturally and denigrated as a highly aggravating way to express yourself.

Since Gorman's article in the '90s, communication experts have given the standard advice to completely avoid this kind of inflection in your own speech, unless you want to bore, annoy, or alienate your listeners. Phrasing statements and questions can understandably make you seem unsure, lacking in confidence, and perhaps even unintelligent.

Many theorists have criticized this criticism itself, suggesting that picking on this perfectly arbitrary vocal variant says more about the critic's hidden sexism or reaction to the lifestyle or culture that they assume it represents.

Dr. Kami Anderson is an interculturalist and linguist and claims that,

> "Uptalk is a lilt that is commonly used to soften communication. It's a way that people use paralanguage, or the sound of their voice and intonations, to appear more friendly, personable, and approachable . . . We begin to perceive the ways in which we show empathy or compassion with our voices as a

weakness, when in actuality it is a demonstration of our ability to consider the perception of others in the workplace. Socialization has indeed made the practice of uptalk more noticeable in women because it is perceived as a gendered communication trait, but . . . that perception is an extension of the workplace practices."

What Anderson is saying, in other words, is that there isn't anything inherently bad about upspeak, except for the fact that it is not considered masculine. But this may be misguided. Studies (Lakoff, 1973, 1975) have found, for example, that people chairing meetings tended to use upspeak three to seven times more often that their subordinates. The conclusion is that upspeak actually has a role in asserting leadership and tends to be used by higher-status individuals. Rather than creating a frame of imposing demands, upspeak establishes an intention of collaboration and ease, which may be just as important in the workplace.

So, should you avoid upspeak or embrace it confidently? Well, as with anything to do with language and communication, the answer is: it depends.

If you are a woman, refusing to apologize for your normal speech patterns is likely to give you a valuable sense of assertiveness and confidence. This also applies to your regional accent and any vocal markers of class or social status—if a certain linguistic idiosyncrasy is yours, then "own" it.

Excellent communicators do not all speak identically, and they are not afraid to be distinctive in the way they speak. However, they do all share the ability to be **conscious** of what they are saying, how they are saying it, and the effect they are having on others. Women do not need to speak like men do in order to be taken seriously. However, if a woman becomes aware that she is coming across as uncertain, unconfident, or nervous, then she can consciously take steps to remedy this. *The key, then, is not whether you use upspeak, but whether your total expression is one of confidence and poise.*

Upspeak, like any vocal style, is likely to become grating if overused. Record yourself and try to spot instances of rising pitch. Experiment with taking those same words and giving them a neutral or even downward inflection at the end. Notice the effect it has on you, your message, and your listener. A little upspeak here and there is probably a good thing and contributes to articulate, varied, and lively tone, but too much can be a bad thing.

The Five Types of Communication Tone

Why exactly is it that upspeak can be such a problem? One reason is that it creates an inappropriate communication tone. **A communication tone is a little like a vocal frame.** It's about how you use words and phrases to establish the kind of communication that can happen. A company will tend to use a more formal tone with shareholders and investors, but adopt a friendlier, more persuasive tone in marketing to its customers. Naturally, the tone we use—our register or the way we "pitch" our message—has a lot to do with the reason we're communicating in the first place. Upspeak, then, can be a problem if it conveys a tone of informality and casualness in a situation that calls for more formality and restraint.

Tone of voice expresses your message, your intention, your feelings . . . but it also affects how people see that message, and the intentions and feelings they ascribe to you. **In essence, there are always two streams of**

information every time we communicate: what we are saying and all the extra data that comes from how we say it.

Type 1: Informative

This is the communication tone that is neutral, objective, and calmly rational. It's the way your doctor speaks to you, or the language of an encyclopedia or service professional. The actual data itself is front and center, not the person sharing that data, or the context, or the relationship between speaker and listener.

Type 2: Humorous

In other words, comedy and fun. Well-paced levity can ease tensions, make you stand out from the crowd, or get your point across quickly. In the wrong place, humor can be disrespectful, unprofessional, or just weird.

Type 3: Respectful

This is a step or two beyond just informative—it's deliberately polite and considerate, seeking to be pleasant, inoffensive, and accommodating. This is almost exclusively the tone of communication between strangers or people in shared public places, where etiquette and social norms stave off the most common misunderstandings or awkwardness.

Type 4: Formal

The kind of tone you find in academic and professional settings. Formal speech uses longer words, longer sentences, and no slang or colloquialisms. Its emphasis is on correctness and a certain portrayal of high standards.

Type 5: Informal

The opposite: a more conversational tone. The voice you use outside of professional situations, either with friends or family.

Miscommunication can occur when we are using a tone that doesn't suit the context or the message, or we are communicating with someone who is using a different tone from ours. For example, you are using an informal and overly familiar tone with an employee you're in the process of disciplining, you are using a humorous tone in a difficult situation with people you don't know well, or you are using a respectful and informative tone when someone has raised a personal grievance with you. **The problem is not the tone but the**

mismatch between the tone and the intention.

Effective communication depends on many different factors—what you're saying, your empathy levels, the platform or medium, and so on—but tone may be the most important. A Grammarly and Harris online poll found that fifty-three percent of knowledge workers felt that the tone of a message was more important than the content. That means that clarity and factual accuracy are only a part of a good message—the way those facts are framed is also important. Furthermore, "intent is not the same as impact"—in other words, simply feeling a certain way means little unless you are able to actually convey that to your listeners.

How can you be more conscious of tone in professional settings?

It can be a difficult balance to strike. Here are a few tips to navigate what can be tricky waters:

Strike a balance between friendly and business-like
Only you will know about your unique workplace culture and context, but try to imagine social niceties and friendliness acting

as a kind of buffer or lubricant. For example, you might make a comment about the weather or ask how a person is, but *for the purpose of* easing into business and quickly warming up before talking more formally. The friendliness is there to assist but is not the main focus. So, that means that a ten-minute conversation about details of your personal life, or an impassioned rant about the weather, is inappropriate.

Be confident but not arrogant
One way to do this is to focus on the content—be clear, calm, and assured in what you're saying, but don't let this turn into *personal* confidence or, even worse, egotism. The surest way to hold your own without conveying a sense of superiority or haughtiness is to show no hesitance in sharing your own opinion or position, but be graceful enough to ask their opinion, request help, or admit that you're wrong, unsure, or don't know.

Aim to be concise but never curt
You can almost always get your message across with fewer words than you think! You're communicating for a reason. What is it? Make sure that you are clear on the crux of your message so that when you deliver it to your audience, you can do so with minimal distraction or irrelevancy. In other words, get

to the point! However, the ordinary conventions of politeness will go a long way in stopping you from coming across as rude or too blunt. Ask questions, say please and thank you, and always add a little buffer before and after what you say, rather than just blurting things out.

Instead of being emotional, be compelling

We've seen that hedging language, upspeak, and using too many crutch words can make you appear weak or overly emotional. You are never required to pretend you don't have feelings or emotions, but a professional and self-regulated person takes on the responsibility of being selective with how they express this emotion. It doesn't matter if you're "right" to feel how you feel—people seldom continue to listen to someone who is overcome with anger, fear, or upset. Instead, make your case with compelling arguments, give your evidence, and be as persuasive as you can. If you're worked up, you may need to take a step back and cool off before deciding what to say and how.

Be genuine but also stay flexible

You need to "be yourself" (in all contexts, not just professional ones), but that doesn't mean that you should relentlessly center your own perspective at the expense of the people you're talking to. You might be a genuinely straight-talking, no-nonsense kind of person, but if the person you're talking to is more nuanced, sensitive, and delicate, then respect that and dial down your tone. You can still be who you are, but be considerate of how the message, the context, and other people may require you to adjust and adapt.

Overall, professionalism is about awareness—it's about knowing that what you say has impact, and deliberately taking steps to speak in a way that gets you what you want while respecting the context and the people you're talking to. Returning to the question of upspeak, then: you may well be perceived as frivolous, uneducated, or annoying if you use upspeak in a professional capacity because it simply does not fit the context. But by the same token, someone who is using an overly stiff and formal communication tone in a casual setting is making the same mistake and showing that they lack situational awareness.

The answer to "What's the best tone to use?" is always "the tone that best matches the context and which will most likely be received by my listeners."

How to Use Signposts

What is the function of road signs when you're driving? They're there to let you know what's coming up, to alert you to exactly where you are, the direction you're going in, and where you're likely to end up if you carry on your route.

Conversational "road signs" serve a similar function. They are verbal and non-verbal markers that tell your listeners what kind of "journey" they're going on, where they are, and where you are taking them. The concept of signposting is most seen in public speaking, where the speaker is expected to move the audience through a sequence of clearly marked key points arranged in a logical argument with clear transitions from one idea to the next. This helps the audience "connect the dots" and see your argument as a whole.

It's easy to forget just how important it is to do this. When you are on your own, the things you already know occupy your mind in a diffuse, all-at-once state. You have already formed your opinions, made your connections, and arrived at your conclusions. It's easy to forget that when you open your mouth to speak to others, *they haven't done all this*. This is why signposting is so important. You need to structure your thoughts and ideas as an organized narrative, with one step leading to the other.

Signposting is commonly thought of as a way to keep your listeners engaged and listening to what you say. But it's more than this. Signposts help your audience come along with you on a cognitive journey so that they can truly *understand*, arriving at your conclusion as a matter of process rather than simply having you tell them some disconnected bits of information. Signposting helps guide listeners through a unique perspective. It helps facilitate their mental processing and categorization of the information you're sharing—and do so in a way that helps make your case.

If you're driving along a road that suddenly ends, splits without warning, or takes you to a surprise destination, you'll feel disoriented or even totally lost. The same thing happens when you signpost incorrectly—and your audience will not want to continue listening to you. In the same way, a long car journey where there are no signs at all and no indication of how far you've gone or what's coming next can lead you to feel bored and irritable. That's why some speakers fail to hold anyone's attention—they've failed to use any signposts.

Now, signposting is not just for people making corporate presentations or keynote speeches. It's for anyone who wants to hold people's attention for longer than two minutes, or tell a good story. The skills are the same. Take a look at the nine most common types of signposts and how to use them.

Transitioning to a New Point

Though you are presenting the audience with a thread of reason that runs all through your argument, you are not just jumping from one idea to the next. You need to signal when you are moving on to a new distinct idea or point, even if it is related to the previous one (and frankly, it should be).

- "Moving on to my second point..."
- "Another separate but related issue is..."
- "Now that I've told you about... I want to switch and talk about..."

Bear in mind that signposts can be verbal but also nonverbal. You can signal a change in idea by switching to a new slide on a presentation; or, in a more casual context, literally listing out points on your fingers; or altering your expression or body language to show that you're changing tack.

Providing More Details on One Point

Help the audience visualize the hierarchy that your ideas fall into so they can easily see which ideas are offered as main themes and which are given as secondary examples, evidence, or counterpoints of those main themes.

- "I now want to say a bit more about..."
- "If we zoom in on..."
- "Taking a closer look at this point here..."

As you can see, many verbal cues are in fact verbal in nature (zoom in, take a look, etc.) and help your audience to visualize.

Linking Similar Points Together

You might need to add a related point to the one you've made already. Make sure you signal that you are giving another point that is distinct, but still related to the previous one, to make sure that people don't think you're broaching an entirely new idea or even offering a counterargument. Don't just make a point—let people know its relationship to the point before it, and to the argument in general.

- "In the same way..."
- "To explain this, we need to understand a second idea..."
- "What that implies is..."

Introducing the Opposite View

It can be extremely disorienting to hear a person go on at length about something that seems to be the opposite of the point they're making. This happens when they don't use a deliberate signpost that signals "I'm about to tell you something different from the main point I'm making." It might seem obvious to you as the speaker, but remember that your listener hasn't arrived there yet, and you have to show them both sides, making it clear that they are, in fact, in opposition.

- "Nevertheless..."
- "On the other hand..."
- "Critics of this line of reasoning tend to say that..."

Changing Topic

It's frustrating when there is no verbal or non-verbal gap in a person's stream of speech, but they have completely switched topic without telling you. If you do this, you risk leaving your audience behind completely and wasting your breath!

"Now, let's consider something completely different..."
"I'd like to pause here and take a look at something else for a moment..."

Changing Topic—But Just for a Moment

When you are reading written words, you can usually see when the author has placed some extra information in brackets. But when you are speaking, you might "open a bracket" and leave your audience hanging and wondering when you will close it again. You need to use signposts to show your listeners that you have taken a temporary detour to express some other loosely connected point, but that you will return again shortly. It's great if you can clearly show what the detour is, why you're making it, how it relates, and how soon you're coming back to the main "road."

- "As a quick side note..."
- "Let me deviate for a minute..."
- "Now, to get back to our original argument..."

Returning to Earlier Points

Repetition can be deathly boring if done out of carelessness or lack of skill, but extremely powerful if done consciously and on purpose. Return only to those points that are genuinely most important—a common technique is to conclude by reiterating the claim you made at the beginning.

- "Because of how important it is, I'll say it again..."
- "To recap..."
- "I'd like to return, then, to what I said earlier..."

Returning to Previous Examples

The same can be done with more specific examples, points of evidence, or little details. The effect can be to draw your listener in and encourage agreement, especially if you incorporate a rhetorical question or question tag:

- "Remember when I mentioned...?"
- "Let's go back to the start of the story, shall we?"
- "You'll remember Frank, who you've already met at the start of the story..."

Summarizing

Naturally, at the end of speaking, you want to pull everything you've said together and present it nicely with a bow on top. The flow of a presentation is usually to present your point, elaborate on it and support it, then summarize it to close. Having a decisive conclusion is a courtesy to the listener, but it also helps you emphasize and reiterate and close in a controlled, deliberate way—the same way you put a period at the end of a sentence.

- "So to wrap up . . ."
- "To summarize all that . . ."
- "To close this off . . ."

Now, while all of this seems pretty clear on paper, there is a knack to doing it well in real life! In a way, a formal presentation in a professional context is easier since we have time to prepare and plan. In more natural, casual conversations, all the same rules apply, but we often have to think on our feet.

Before we end this chapter (isn't *that* a nice signpost?), let's consider one bad habit that will totally destroy other people's willingness to listen to you. Have you ever been socializing and felt yourself trapped in a "conversation" with someone who simply would not stop talking? It's as though once they opened their mouths, they could not physically close it again. You felt bored, irritated, and desperate to run away. Why? Poor signposting.

To make sure that *you're* not being this person (and yes, you could be, considering how seldom anyone actually tells someone else "you're boring me to tears"), pay attention to the structure of what you're saying. Even if you only speak for fifteen seconds, what you say needs to have a main point, it needs to be introduced, supported, or expanded on in some way, then concluded. If you don't, you risk trapping you both in a never-ending story.

Avoid:

"Going off on a tangent"—Does the piece of information *directly* relate to your main point? Leave it out. If you insist on saying it, wait your turn to speak next and launch a different, separate thread.

Repeating the same material—Say what you need to, say it once with a little expansion, then drop it. Your listeners heard you!

Starting the story too early—If you want to tell someone about an interesting person you met, don't start the story a month before when you were reading a book that reminded you to go to an event that you went to and met someone, who then in turn introduced you to the second person... Just start at the point you met them.

Carrying the story on for too long—Have a clear idea of where the "punchline" is. Once you've made your point, don't then get tempted to start up a fresh idea or expand some auxiliary point. It will feel like you're overstaying your welcome, so to speak.

Delving into pointless detail and rebuttal—If you dwell too long on some minor detail of the story, it's as though the car has stalled on the journey. Your listeners will simply register you as having gotten distracted from telling your own story, and they'll stop paying attention. Similarly, don't get too carried away entertaining every little possible variant or argument against what you're saying—you don't have all day!

If you've ever been accused of "talking too much," rest assured that you *can* become a better storyteller. It's about quality, not quantity. The irony is that it's usually when we feel that people aren't listening that we tend to do worse with signposting and structuring our speech. But the truth is that if you are clear and organized and have enough consideration to deliver your message in a digestible form for your audience, they will often return this consideration by listening to you for a lot longer than you'd think.

Summary:

- A few crutch words like *um*, *ah*, *well*, *you know*, *like*, *so*, *right*, and *okay* are natural, but too many can undermine your credibility and make it more difficult to understand you. Instead, become aware of the habit and consciously replace crutch words and empty language with confident silence. Being calm and thoughtful shows consideration for your audience and gets your point across more effectively.
- Likewise try to avoid hedging or softening language and instead be clear, concise, and confident in your expression.
- Your communication tone is like a vocal frame you set, so pay attention to whether you are being informative, humorous, respectful, formal, or informal. No tone is wrong, but a mismatch between tone and intention, or tone and context, can be a problem.
- Be especially conscious of upspeak (making statements with the intonation that belongs to questions), and ask whether it may be damaging your credibility or interfering with your message.

- With tone, strike a balance between friendly and business-like, confident and arrogant, concise and curt, emotional and merely compelling, and so on. Professionalism is about awareness and deliberately taking steps to speak in a way that gets you what you want while respecting the context and your audience.
- Especially with public speaking, use signposts—which are verbal and non-verbal markers that tell your listeners what kind of "journey" they're going on, where they are, and where you are taking them. Use a signpost every time you want to transition, give further detail, link points, change topics, offer a counterpoint, or summarize.

Chapter 3: Painting with Words

The Art of Vivid Language: Use Imagery and Rhythm

Whether you're speaking to one person or an entire audience, if you want your listeners to really absorb what you say to them, paint them a picture . . . that is, help them paint their own *mental* picture of what you're saying. Verbal expression is a fundamentally human characteristic, but long before we evolved even this, we processed our world in pictures via five senses deeply embedded in the real, physical world. That means that if we can talk in such a way as to address and engage this pre-verbal world of imagery and sensation, we allow ourselves to connect with other people on a deeper level.

This is what vivid language does, and visual imagery and rhythm (sight and sound) are two powerful components. Those who are naturally talented speakers find themselves drawing on these extra-verbal skills without consciously realizing it. But once you're aware of how to do so deliberately, you might find that a whole world of expression opens up to you, and you instantly become a more compelling, relatable, and vibrant speaker.

How to Paint the Picture

All words are representations of ideas, but, as they say, a picture paints a thousand words. **Images are richer and work more quickly and more effectively on listeners.** Using imagery can actually bypass language in a way, and transmit information that feels closer to lived experience, and not just something that someone is telling you about. To get a hang of using imagery in conversation, you need to master the use of three tools:

1. Concreteness
2. Simile
3. Metaphor

Concreteness is about being embedded in the world, about being real. You can define a technical term a million different ways, but the moment you give someone an example of what you're talking about, they will instantly understand it on a deeper, more tangible level. Many highly skilled orators (like politicians or motivational speakers) will make abstract theories and concepts instantly relatable by boiling them down into real terms—instead of talking about the economy, they talk about people sitting around a kitchen table doing the family budget. They talk about specific people, specific places, and real events. In the same way that emotional responses are processed more quickly in the brain than rational ones, things we can touch, see, smell, etc. are processed more easily and more quickly than symbols and abstractions.

Simile is one way that we can tether an abstraction to something else—usually something less abstract. It's a comparison that usually uses *like* or *as*. For example:

"It was like a kick in the teeth."
"As easy as pie."
"They descended on the buffet like a plague of locusts."

Metaphor is another way to tether abstract to concrete and make illuminating comparisons. An oft-repeated metaphor that many of us will remember from school is the classic "the mitochondria is the powerhouse of the cell." Metaphors directly state that something *is* something else in order to compare two different but related ideas or objects. The mitochondria metaphor works because none of us have actually seen mitochondria, and the way in which they generate energy is rather complex and vague.

However, if a teacher tells you it's like a powerhouse, you very quickly and clearly understand the message: This is a part of the cell that generates energy. The concrete has been tethered to the abstract, of which you now have a better grasp. For proof of how impactful metaphors can be, ask yourself how much of the mitochondria's technical functioning you can remember from school—not much right? But if you're told once that it is a powerhouse, you're likely to remember that little detail for the rest of your life.

Concrete similes and metaphors add power and depth to what you're saying. Depending on how extreme the comparison is (i.e., how unalike the two things are in real life), you can inject enormous color into what you're saying, giving ideas a positive or negative spin (think about the effect of calling cigarettes "coffin nails"), evoking a particular emotion, or even adding a dose of humor.

Consider the funny story tells of how Keats and Shakespeare were arguing in heaven over who was the best wordsmith. They agreed to spontaneously compose some poetry/prose to describe the next person who walked over the hill. When a man with severe rickets emerged, Keats looked at the very bent legs and hesitated before saying,

"See over the hill there strode
A man whose legs are very bowed."

This was well and good, but then it was Shakespeare's turn, who said,

"Alas what manner of man is this,
who carries his balls in parenthesis?"

And Keats had to admit that Shakespeare was, after all, the superior wordsmith!

Other ways to add color and depth to your language:

- Use imaginative adjectives. Forget about "nice" or "beautiful" and try to use more specific, unique words—they will stick in the listener's memory, and even if they don't understand the word, you may still come across as intelligent and erudite.

- Use the power of detail. This is not unlike zooming in and zooming out again with chunking. You could speak for forty minutes about how you struggled for money in your youth and how it made you the resilient, light-hearted person you are today. Or you could just say, "Growing up we were so poor, we went to KFC to lick other people's fingers."
- Be a little unexpected. When people hear cliches, they stop thinking. Instead be fresh in the way you describe things and don't be afraid to say something that will make people sit up and say, "Wait, what?"

Rhythm and How to Go with the Flow

Most people think of music as soon as they hear the word "rhythm." There's good reason for this—**language is musical by nature, and so much of the meaning it conveys comes down to its rate, its articulation, its flow, and the way it moves through time**. Rhythm is the way that sounds or words repeatedly change in a regular fashion. When someone strikes a drum in a periodic way, we "tune into" this beat, allowing ourselves to sync up with it, predicting the next beat and thus feeling as though we are somehow aligned. It's the same when people speak: If someone is delivering their message with a repeated, consistent rhythm, it provides a kind of aural scaffolding onto which we can sync, our comprehension is deeper, and we are more engrossed.

For example, if they speak quickly and with rapid-fire sentences, we might feel alert, even a little anxious and hurried. If they repeat certain phrases over and over, and every point they make is delivered using the same sentence structure, we start to be almost lulled into that rhythm ourselves, coming through sheer repetition into line with the message being shared. Take a look at a few ways you can consciously control the rhythm of your speech to achieve certain effects.

Parallelism

That is to say, *grammatically* parallel, i.e., the structure of the sentences are repeated or equivalent in some way. This is typically done when you are listing out things—even just two things. Using parallelism can make your message feel more coherent and convincing, and you may seem a lot more conscious and in control as a result.

Consider both these sentences:

Give me liberty or give me death.
Give me liberty or death.

The difference may seem small, but there is one, isn't there? Though they say precisely the same thing, the first one seems more solid somehow. Consider also:

Better to rule in hell than to serve in heaven.
Better to be a ruler in hell than to serve in heaven.

Again, the meaning is essentially the same, but in the first sentence, both clauses take the same form—rule in heaven is compared to serve in hell. The structure is mirrored, and so the expression feels more fluid. The second mixes two forms and the effect is lost. If, however, it were changed to "better to be a ruler in hell than to be a slave in heaven" it would be parallel and sound better. Finally, consider the form of individual words themselves:

I love skiing, painting, and my dog.
I love skiing, painting, and walking my dog.

Can you see how in the first sentence, the expression feels disjoined because one thing in the list (dog) is not like the other two? Even if only unconsciously, a listener may perceive this lack of coherence and organization and ascribe it to your overall message. Use parallelism when you can—even if it's only in small ways—and your speech will feel more whole, more connected, and stronger.

Repetition

Closely related to this is repetition, which you might end up doing when using parallelism (for example, consider the repetition of "give me" in the example above). There is a definite tendency for the human mind to assume that the things it is exposed to repeatedly must somehow be truer (psychologists call this the illusory truth effect). That's why if you want to convince or persuade your audience, or even just drill a point home so they can really grasp it, then you'll need to repeat your message more than once.

Repetition is a little like putting text in bold underline—it tells people what is important, and it helps you structure your ideas by summarizing and synthesizing main ideas. In many ways, it's also a way to incorporate parallelism, resulting in a message that not only "sounds right" but is more easily understood. Think about Winston Churchill's famous "we shall fight them on the beaches" speech:

> We shall go on to the end. We shall fight in France, we shall fight on the seas and oceans, we shall fight with growing confidence and growing strength in the air, we shall defend our island, whatever the cost may be. We shall fight on the beaches, we shall fight on the landing grounds, we shall fight in the fields and in the streets, we shall fight in the hills; we shall never surrender.

This section came at the very end of a long and impassioned speech filled with so much other rousing imagery, that by the time the crowds heard this section, the almost literal drumbeat repetition of *we shall fight, we shall fight, we shall fight* left them in awed silence. Conservative member of parliament Chips Channon later said that "he was eloquent and oratorical and used magnificent English; several Labour members cried." Churchill's speech is regarded as a masterpiece of oration, precisely because it was able to stir the emotions so far beyond the purview of ordinary language that it was more like poetry or music.

Alliteration and Assonance

Alliteration is really a form of repetition, but what is repeated is single sounds and letters, in this case consonants. Alliteration works best when the repeated sounds actually connect in some meaningful way with the message itself. For example, "the girl read a book by a babbling brook" repeats the "b" sound and, consequently, emphasizes the bubbling sound of the water, painting a subtle picture. In Shakespeare's "fair is foul and foul is fair: hover through the fog and filthy air," the repetition of the "f" sound almost seems to become the filthy fog itself.

In your own speech, you don't need to get too carried away or it will feel forced. Just be aware always that the literal sound of the words you choose is also part of the message. If you really want to emphasize your negative opinion of a character, you might say so much more by calling him "slimy and sleezy" than if you had just called him "a shady guy."

Assonance, on the other hand, repeats vowel sounds and letters within words, rather than at the beginning. Some examples are "free as a breeze" (can you almost hear someone saying *wheee*?) and "no pain, no gain." When using either alliteration or assonance, remember that a little goes a long way. Don't overdo it or the effect may feel a little trite!

How to Be a Masterful Storyteller

Have you ever tried to tell a joke and sadly watched as it fell flat? Or maybe someone else was trying to tell you such a joke, and somehow bungled the delivery.

Think carefully about exactly *why* the joke failed. One obvious reason is that the punchline was mangled or the logic and flow of the story was disrupted somehow. But a far more likely reason was that the joke failed to evoke the right emotions.

A joke is just a very short story that is meant to evoke a small set of reactions (humor, shock), but it tells us a lot about the way **human beings react not just to "information" but to narrative. They do this not solely by having a cognitive grasp on what they're told, but on making an emotional connection to it.** Those who understand this process end up being the proverbial good storytellers, and it's a very rarified art, indeed.

Even if you aren't literally telling a joke or delivering a classic story to an audience, you will at some point need to incorporate storytelling in your communication. Perhaps you have to give a work presentation, convince someone of your viewpoint, flirt and get someone to like you, summon up some compassion for yourself when you've done something wrong, inspire someone to act, make a complicated argument for something, or simply tell people about what you did on the weekend without boring them to tears!

As you can imagine, good storytelling is not just about words, but also how we use our voice, body language, gestures, facial expressions, and even visual aids. Let's look at how.

Tip 1: Use stories to support what you're saying

Consider a story a tool. Give your audience an example of what you're talking about, or show them a story that quickly captures or demonstrates the point you're making. You don't need to explain *why* you have told the story, however: People will intuitively grasp it and make their own conclusions (and become more engaged in the process).

For example, if you wanted to create a feeling of rapport and make yourself seem relatable and real, you might share a touching story from your childhood that would resonate with anyone. If you wanted to quickly explain the rather complex view you have on commitment to one's dreams, you could quickly tell a little story about the difference between a chicken and a pig when it comes to bacon and eggs (punchline: "the chicken is involved, but the pig is really *committed*!"). Another way to use stories is to have them introduce a certain point. Perhaps you want to answer a question about what you do for work by explaining how one day, you started to wonder if there was a better way to chop an avocado . . .

The best stories are those that quickly make their point and directly speak to our emotional experiences or our five senses. Use metaphor, simile, and vivid language to make complex topics seem more accessible. Finally, ensure your audience can draw links between the story and the current situation, by saying something like, "And that goes to show . . ." or "after that day everything changed," and so on.

Tip 2: Set the scene, present the tale

All of us instinctively know what a good story is—we knew it even when we were children! To tell a compelling story, you'll need to do the same. Give some background context by telling your audience when and where the story took place. Bear in mind this is just to briefly sketch the stage the story unfolds on, so to speak—don't get distracted on these details or worry too much about accuracy. If the weather, for example, doesn't really feature in the story, don't bother mentioning it at length.

Another tip is to deliver your story with a slight increase in volume than you ordinarily would be used to. People will register this and pay closer attention—we can't help it! Once you have their attention, however, keep it by being careful with your pace. Don't go too fast (i.e., because you're nervous and worried about holding their interest) or too slow (people will resent it and stop paying attention). Instead, imagine that you're delivering interesting nuggets of information at a uniform pace. You can pause and slow down a little on purpose to heighten anticipation, but only do so if you will then release that tension by revealing a big payoff at the end.

Keep your speech varied and dynamic. Modulate your voice between high and low pitch, high and low volume, and varying sentence lengths and structures. You can even use rhetorical questions to draw people in and encourage them along the main beats of the story. This is the meaning of being articulate—

being able to speak with ease and flexibility the same way a gymnast moves with ease and flexibility through their routine. Depending on the situation, you might find it useful to almost play the parts of different roles in the story—subtly change your voice, accent, facial expression, or way of speaking when delivering the lines of a speaker in the story.

Tip 3: Keep it short

Brevity is the sole of wit. A short, pithy story has the greatest chance of impacting your listener and staying with them long afterward. A short story is easier to digest and simpler to understand. This is not to say that you can't have success telling longer stories (after all, people love things like TED talks) but that you will need to work harder to maintain people's attention. Consistently imagine yourself in the other person's shoes. They will always be listening *for a reason*; they'll be primed and on the lookout to spot the lesson, the punchline, or the big idea. If you make them wait for it, or bury it somewhere underneath loads of irrelevant detail, they may give up listening and decide the payoff is not worth it.

Tip 4: Make it mean something

Human beings love stories, but not because they are merely entertaining. It's the way people have transmitted meaning and value for all of human history. Stories are told to make points, to convince, to pass down wisdom, to warn, to teach, to make the complicated easier to understand . . . and yes, occasionally to entertain.

It's a good idea to try to embed your story in some larger framework of meaning. What did you learn from the anecdote you just shared? What did this event teach you? How did life change because of this story? What does it all mean? In a persuasive presentation, you can indulge a lot in suggesting an interpretation for your listeners; in more casual contexts it's usually better to hint at the "moral of the story" rather than lecture too much. In traditional cultures, storytellers are lauded not when they have good yarns to tell, but when they are best able to "prescribe" the right story for the right listener, as though it were medicine. Know your audience and the kind of narrative they are likely to respond to, and you will speak to them on deeper level.

Tip 5: Start with a bang

A "hook" is what it sounds like—something to grab ahold of your audience. The sooner you have a hook to catch them, the better. It's almost always a good idea to start with your main point, or at least strongly hint at it. Consider the opening lines of Jane Austen's *Pride and Prejudice*: "It is a truth universally acknowledged, that a single man in possession of a good fortune, must be in want of a wife." This is not only a great hook, it's also a single-sentence summary of the entire novel's central theme. Then there's George Orwell's *1984*, which opens with *"*It was a bright cold day in April, and the clocks were striking thirteen.*"* Immediately the audience is given a question to mull over—what kind of world is this?

Of course, these are novels with authors who have had time to think about these first lines. When telling a story on the spur of the moment, you can still be impactful, however, simply by remembering that you need to start with something that will immediately catch attention. One clever way of doing this is to actively downplay something that is quite absurd: "Oh? I didn't tell you about the time a crocodile ate my lunchbox? Well, the first thing you need to understand was that I never liked that lunchbox anyway . . ."

To do this effectively, you need to understand the story in full for yourself before you open your mouth. There's nothing worse than someone who starts telling you a story and halfway through it's clear that they don't know where they're going with it (or worse, when to stop!). Every story needs to be a concise, self-contained entity that has a beginning, middle and end. Even if it's not a joke, it needs a "punchline." Knowing the main point will help you identify key "beats" or story points along the way and stay on track. But remember: these beats are not a list of dry, objective facts. They are a carefully curated string of *emotional experiences*. You describe the day (it was hot, your legs were sticking to the car seat) and how excited you were (you show this excitement in your facial expression, voice, and posture). The girl of your dreams waltzed up to you and smiled, and it was like an angel had spoken (simile) ... These are all emotional nuggets rather than data points!

Some final hints and tricks:

A story can be interesting and true, but if it's not **relevant** to the listener or to you or your message, don't tell it. In ordinary conversation, unless encouraged to do so, never tell a story that is longer than about a minute (this, by the way, is quite a long time).

If a particular detail is not intrinsic to the logic of the story, leave it out entirely. ("It was Thursday and that was when he usually had his spin class, but that day the class was canceled because the instructor had broken her toe last weekend at the carnival. You know, the one they're hosting to raise funds for that church thing we saw in the paper. Anyway, that's why he was free on *that* Thursday even though he ordinarily wouldn't have been, so he bumped into my friend . . ." It's easier to just say "One day, he bumped into her.")

When rehearsing for a presentation, record or film yourself first and do practice runs—many people are surprised to see that they need to stand up taller, speak more slowly, and breathe more deeply! Finally, gauge reactions as you go and adjust your story in real time. If you realize that the other person is not familiar with the TV show/book/idea you're talking about, then stop talking about it!

Summary:

- If you want your listeners to really absorb what you say to them, paint them a mental picture. Do this by using vivid and concrete imagery, similes (using *like* or *as*), and metaphors to connect abstract ideas with

more real-world ones. Use adjectives and interesting details and be a little unexpected.
- Language is musical by nature, and much of the meaning it conveys comes down to its rate, its articulation, its flow, and the way it moves through time. Pay attention to the rhythm and flow of your speech.
- In parallelism, we repeat certain structures to create an effect. Repetition drives our point home and makes it seem more true, as do alliteration (repetition of initial consonant sounds) and assonance (repetition of internal or vowel sounds).
- Human beings react not just to "information" but to narrative; to be a good storyteller, you need to go beyond sharing information and facts, and help your listeners form an emotional connection to what you're saying. Good stories enlist the use of our voice, body language, gestures, facial expressions, and even visual aids.
- Make sure that your story illustrates supports or connects to your larger point or circumstance. Set the scene but don't dawdle on unnecessary detail. Start with a bang and keep things at a moderate pace, being concise. Be relevant and interesting,

and if you can, practice your story ahead of time!

Chapter 4: Communication's Most Underrated Skill

Asking the Right Questions

Communication is certainly about what you say and how you say it. But that's only fifty percent of the conversation, right? In this chapter, we'll take a closer look at the important but sadly overlooked skills of listening, asking questions, and allowing the other person to shine during conversations. Becoming a better communicator is not the same as becoming a better public speaker. Knowing how to carefully present your ideas is only one half of the story—your listener is the other half, and unless they are on board, you will only ever be engaging in a monologue, not a dialogue.

One of the easiest and most natural ways to connect with the other person is to just ask questions. So many poor communicators could instantly improve by doing this alone.

But asking the *right* questions is also important. What's more, you need to pay special attention to how you ask them and when. Mastering the questioning process means you gather more and better-quality information, you build stronger connections with others, you inspire trust and liking, you learn, and you may even find yourself being helpful in someone else's learning process. In short, good questions allow you to access the best that communication can be.

Have you ever been in a conversation where it felt you were being interrogated? Think back to a memory like this, or just imagine what that kind of scene would look like. Now, what are the kind of questions that an interrogator asks?

Did you do it?
Where were you the night of the eleventh?
You knew the victim, right?

All of the above are closed questions—meaning they have only one short possible answer. Yes or no, or some other tiny, single-word snippet of information. A closed question is like a little dart that demands only one specific kind of information from the other person. It's closed because, in effect, it closes the whole world of potential answers down, usually just to one or two options. Consequently, it closes the conversation itself down. Once you answer a closed question, there's very little else for you to do.

If you use only closed questions in conversation, you risk coming across as an interrogator, because others will feel that you are deliberately and forcefully closing off avenues in this way. The other person will rightly feel that they are sitting there at your mercy, being probed. It's not fun, and it usually peters out pretty quickly.

That said, closed questions have their uses, too:

- You can use them to confirm your understanding of what you've been told ("So you were a history major, then, right?")
- You can use them to make conclusions or summaries of what's been discussed so far ("So we've all agreed to never go to McDonalds for lunch again, right?")

- You can also use them as part of frame setting, i.e., to set the tone and scope of a more formal or structured conversation ("Were you satisfied with your service at McDonald's today?")

Imagine closed questions like periods in a sentence—you only need a few, but when used correctly, they help structure your sentences and give you a pause now and then. Use too many and everything will feel too rapid fire and staccato.

In what situations can we use open-ended questions? That question itself is a good example of one! We are opening the range of possible answers, and in so doing, opening up the conversation. We are inviting the other person into the mix and allowing them to have a turn at directing the conversation's course. Open-ended questions show curiosity and interest in the other person, without allowing assumptions and prejudices to pre-select what we already think the answers will be.

Open-ended questions allow you to:

- Develop and extend a conversation, expanding on a point or deepening your grasp of it ("So what exactly made you so

interested in the medieval period in the first place?")
- Flesh out an idea or concept and find out more details about it ("What other specific budgeting issues do we want to discuss in the meeting on Friday?")
- Probe for opinions and unique perspectives ("From your point of view, what do you think went wrong with this program?")

As you can probably see, good conversational flow contains *both* open and closed questions.

How to Use Funnel Questions

Funnel questions are what they sound like: questions that guide information in increasing detail down a narrowing path. Like a funnel, the process begins wide and broad with open questions, and steadily narrows to a point with closed questions. Each question leads on from the last, but is a little more narrowed in scope, becoming progressively more closed and detailed.

Using such a technique, you ease the other person into answering more direct and specific questions, while balancing this with invitations to supply additional information as they go. Because it strikes a balance between probing/interrogating and genuine conversation, this technique is most often used in occupational settings—for example, job interviews.

Imagine that an interviewer attempts first to put the interviewee at ease by asking very general open-ended questions—how they are, whether they found the journey to the office okay, etc. This soothes any tension. Slowly and gradually, the interviewer leads, in increments, to more and more targeted questions:

So how are you finding this amazing Californian sunshine?
I hope the big move is going well—what's the new neighborhood like?
Great. So, if I recall correctly, your previous job was in our branch in Minnesota. Can you give me a rundown of your time there?
I'm interested in hearing more about your work with fundraising around that time.
Can you tell me more about the team members?
Can I ask how much you were able to raise?

You can see the funnel at work if you attempt to answer these questions—you'll see that the answers will get progressively shorter but more specific as they go, responding with something like "Eight hundred thousand dollars" at the end. Importantly, this is an easier and gentler way to ask such questions; consider how uncomfortable it would have been to ask the final question first. The interviewee might have felt put on the spot or interrogated, whereas with some "warm-up" questions that naturally lead from one to the other, this question is not likely to feel like an imposition.

Here's a summary of how to ask funnel questions:

1. Begin with open-ended questions

Think of these not even as questions but as invitations to share information—as the other person wishes to share it.

2. Ask for additional explanation

Ask for clarification based on the answer to the above question. These are questions that help you understand the motivations, reasoning, and cause/effect relationships behind certain situations, as well the person's perspective on it all. You're not merely being polite and making small talk—you use the answers you're given to inform your next questions.

3. Ask for more details according to what you're told

Narrow the funnel one step at a time. You might ask for examples, justifications, explanations, or more specific instances or pieces of evidence or support. Take another step closer to the specific information you're looking for. This may require just one question or it can take many, depending on the topic.

4. Finally, reverse the funnel

This final step is optional, but you can also start working the funnel in reverse again, using the very detailed answer you got to inspire another funnel that begins with broad questions again. For example, after you're told that the fundraising team generated eight hundred thousand dollars, you can immediately sit back in your chair and say, "Okay, that's impressive. How did you do that?" The conversation continues with you getting the information you want, but without badgering or leading the other person.

Funnel questions are not only for formal or professional situations, however. They can be used any time you are trying to extract some information from someone, but in a way that is easy, comfortable, and personable. A psychiatrist, for example, might need to find out whether a patient had suicidal thoughts, but this is a difficult question to ask, and so it's best to lead into it with a long series of funnel questions. The psychiatrist doesn't rush through the conversation, and genuinely listens to answers (i.e., doesn't give the impression that they are "hunting" down just one desired response). Gently, the psychiatrist keeps zoning in on those aspects of the patient's answer that will most likely lead to ideas around depression and suicide. Near the end of the funnel, the psychiatrist begins to use words like "specifically" and "exactly" to continue narrowing down. But with the psychiatrist's inviting, encouraging language and a genuine desire to listen, the patient never feels manipulated or hurried along, and the psychiatrist gets the information they want.

In your own conversations, whoever you're speaking to and whatever information you're trying to get, keep the image of a funnel in mind. Never make sharp jumps from very general to very specific—and always lead gently from one into the other.

How You Structure a Question Matters

It goes without saying that the question you ask determines the answer you get. But when you really grasp what this means, you understand just how much of a difference question structure can make. Ask a poor question and you get a poor answer!

Take a look at these different question types/forms and notice how their structure influences the kind of answer you might get:

Probing questions

That is, questions that get right to the core of the matter. These are typically closed questions and are more direct, targeted, and focused, often using "narrowing language" such as *exactly* or *specifically*, or else uses question words that inspire a single answer—when, where, who.

"Exactly how much will it cost if we want to send the whole office the course?"
"When is the latest I can get back to you on this?"
"What evidence do we currently have that the diagnosis made at the time was correct?"

(Notice in this last instance that the question is probing without necessarily being closed).

Leading questions

As though you are taking the other person by the hand and pulling them along with you on your train of thought—which isn't always as bad as it sounds! There are a few ways to do this.

- **By making an assumption**—"How much will you be willing to invest in your wellbeing today?" (Assumption: you are in fact going to invest!). "What did I do wrong here?" (Assumption: I have actually done something wrong). Note that this is one way that a frame is created—the frame is built up on "shared" assumptions.
- **By deliberately asking for agreement, compliance, or support**—"It's expensive, don't you think?" or "I think we both want the same thing here, right?" Even if the other person doesn't feel compelled to verbally respond, you are still leading them, and the focus is still on them coming along with you.
- **By making your desired answer the easiest one**—Let's say you want someone to say yes. You could say, "Shall we have a break?" and be far more likely to receive that yes than if you asked, "Shall we pause here or continue on?" The latter question is psychologically felt as offering two fifty-

fifty options, whereas with the former, the easier response seems just to agree/nod/say yes. In the same vein, asking, "It's noon—what do you want to do now?" is the question least likely to have the other person spontaneously agree to a break like you want them to.
- **By presenting two "options"**—the key here, of course, is that you're happy with either option! Technically and logically, they *can* say "neither," but they may instead default to choosing one of the two you have presented.

Rhetorical Questions

As we all know, rhetorical questions aren't actually questions at all, but statements that are made in such a way as to encourage and elicit agreement. For example, "Isn't this new layout so much easier to work with?" Strictly speaking, this isn't a question form, but rather something you are dressing up as a question in order to frame it as something you are seeking their agreement on, rather than just *telling* them. If you just say, "The new layout is better," you are potentially inviting disagreement or simply stating a personal opinion, and the other person's perspective is irrelevant. If you make it a rhetorical question, however, you are signaling that you are *not* simply telling someone, but acknowledging the value of them being in agreement with you—it's halfway between arguing that you're right and politely asking for their agreement!

To conclude, here are a few tips for using questions in a proactive, conscious way:

- Whatever you do, don't forget to ask questions entirely—even poorly formatted questions are better than none at all!
- Want to create a feeling of rapport or develop a conversation? Use open-ended questions.
- Want to get particular information out of a person? Use probing questions or closed questions—so long as they are at the end of a funnel!
- Want to persuade someone, close a deal, or make a sale? Use leading and rhetorical questions.
- In conversations of all kinds, make sure you are mixing things up—don't have three questions of all one type right after one another, for example.

How to Be a Truly Effective Listener

Many people *think* they are good listeners. Few of them are right!

Being an effective listener is about so much more than comprehending what you're told, or simply behaving in a way to make it appear that you are paying attention. In an attempt to be better communicators, many of us will begin with our side of things and try to improve the way we speak; the truth is that you can drastically improve all your relationships by starting on the other side and becoming an excellent listener first.

Good listening is actually a collection of different skills: It's about hearing, understanding, interpreting, and responding, and it's something that we do *with* someone as the conversation unfolds in time. A good mindset shift is to realize that listening well is primarily about the other person—you know you have truly listened if your listening has created an outcome that the other person intended and wanted.

The HURIER Method

Judi Brownell from Cornell University created the acronym HURIER to help people remember the key skills behind masterful listening: Hearing, Understanding, Remembering, Interpreting, Evaluating, and Responding. Here are the components of Brownell's model:

H: Hearing

Here, "hearing" means any and all processes that result in you acquiring new information through your senses, and can include things like sight and touch as well as sound. Good listeners can synthesize information on all these channels; it's what makes us say "I hear you" when we are in fact responding to emotions implied in facial expressions, gestures, and posture. Even when it does come to auditory sensation, there is a lot to listen for beyond the basic facts of the message. You can hear the tone, pace, pitch, volume, and articulation of the voice. You can hear the accent, the rate and depth of breath, and the little clues that hint at certain emotions.

To really hear someone, make sure that it's the only thing you're doing. Don't multitask or daydream about what you'll say once they stop talking. Don't get distracted by devices or passersby. Just sit in the person's presence and be receptive to what they're sharing, without needing to hurry or rush them through to a conclusion. If you really can't give them your full attention, there's nothing wrong with postponing the conversation until a time when you can.

Example: You're catching up with an old-school friend you haven't seen in ten years. You sit somewhere quiet and give him your absolute full attention, noticing the subtly different accent he now has, the slight tiredness in his voice, and the fact that he's speaking quite slowly. He is telling you a story about a new promotion at work, and you notice his voice speeds up and gets a little formal as he does so.

U: Understanding

Naturally, you want to comprehend the *meaning* of what you're told once you carefully receive and absorb it. Making sense of what you're told is a process that starts with them and ends with you as you put together the pieces of information they've shared.

Once a message leaves its sender and floats across the void in order to reach the listener, there are countless ways for things to be lost or distorted. One of the worst things you can do as a listener is to assume you have heard and understood when you haven't. Consider how a certain word or phrase may mean slightly different things to them than they do to you because of cultural or generational differences. Consider how differently they may use certain imagery, cultural references, or even what they consider to be courteous and good-mannered.

Luckily, this is precisely what communication is for—to close these gaps and dissolve these potential misunderstandings. Check in with the other person to see whether the version of their message you've received is something they recognize. If you're not clear on something, ask for clarification. Paraphrase what you've been told, saying, "Have I got that right?" Take your time and ask questions rather than assume you know certain details, and importantly, don't interrupt people as they speak—you might miss out on crucial information.

Example: He's summarizing the last ten years of his work for his company, and you're missing some of the details since you're not familiar with his industry. You ask him at one point, "So you say you're a consultant now but actually you're still technically employed by them, right?" You're not only trying to understand what this word "consultant" means to him linguistically but also emotionally.

R: Remembering

It is a mistake to think of listening as "passive." As you listen, you are holding all the details of what you're told and actively assembling them as you go, collaboratively creating the meaning with the other person. To do this, you need to be able to recall what you've been told earlier. That may mean details from five minutes ago, or it can mean something you were told last year. Not only does effective listening require you to remember details, it requires that you put these details together.

If you think, "But my memory is terrible," then don't worry—most problems with remembering during conversations are actually not about memory but about *attention*. You usually "forget" something not because your memory is bad, but because you weren't properly attending to the stimulus in the first place. To improve your memory, simply slow down, pay close attention, and actively link everything you're told with everything you've already been told right there in the moment. You can then use this to inspire further questions or requests for clarification.

Example: He starts talking about his family, and you think: Hang on, he's telling me now about *his sister . . . but which sister was that? So you say, "That's so interesting! I remember you mentioned your sister when we spoke on the phone last week. Is this the same sister?" He says, "Oh, no, this is my younger sister." You make a mental note that he has (at least!) two sisters. This little interlude will fill in any of your own memory gaps **and** make it appear that you are an attentive, careful listener.*

I: Interpreting

The first three letters explain how you receive information and consciously connect it with other information, and in so doing deepen your comprehension of what it all means. From that point, naturally, you can't help but interpret the message. It's as though we zoom out a little and look at everything around the message—the context, the speaker (their biases, goals, expectations, etc.), the additional nonverbal information being shared, any hidden subtext, and so on. These things can add depth and richness to a message, or they can even change a message completely into something else.

Note *everything* you can observe about what the person in front of you is communicating:

- Their nonverbal cues such as body language, voice characteristics, expression, and so on
- The underlying emotional meaning behind their words
- The context of the conversation and why it is happening
- How the other person may be responding to you
- The speaker's personality, biases, blind spots, and style of expression
- Cultural, generational, gender, or even socioeconomic factors

Example: You notice an overwhelming emotion of stress and exhaustion in your old school friend, and how his new professional demands and commitments seem to have changed the way he speaks. You note how all of this comes together with a somewhat shy but intense personality, and you observe his style of dress—very somber and businesslike but quite expensive clothing.

E: Evaluating

Once you've gathered all of this data together, the next step is obviously to decide what to do with it. Crucially, this comes at the end, not the beginning, so you can make sure you're in possession of the *entire* message before coming to any conclusions. Now, evaluating does **not** mean you decide whether you believe the person, whether you like them or what they're saying, or whether you agree. This is not a question of judgment but rather appraisal. Here we need to be on guard against our own assumptions and prejudices. Too many of us are too quick to jump into this stage before we've given the other person the chance to express their full message, or ourselves the chance to properly and thoughtfully digest it. Keep reminding yourself that there is no rush, and you don't even have to come to an evaluation if you don't yet feel you're ready.

Example: You start to conclude that your friend's work and occupational status has become a big part of his identity. Though he is very casually telling you about his life, and idly complaining about being overworked, you wonder if part of him relishes the label of "workaholic" and if in some subtle way he is showing off. This, however, is a temporary theory, and you don't jump to conclusions just yet. What's more, you acknowledge that much of this interpretation may come from your own values around work and money, your history with this friend in school, and the fact that you used to be a little competitive back then ...

Keep an open mind. Listen to what they're saying, not what you might think they're saying or what you wish they were saying. This is the stage where a little neutral judgment and objectivity can go a long way. You don't have to be emotionless, just be clear about what it emotion and what is logic. Recognize your ideas as separate from theirs, and identify any influence from biases, beliefs and values—whether theirs or your own. Finally, make a clear distinction between the speaker and the message they're sharing. Listening means hearing the message—not jumping to conclusions that fit in line with our assumptions about who the person is or should be.

R: Responding

The very last step is to respond. Yet, how many of us jump in to respond before the other person has even finished speaking? We skip right over the understanding, the remembering, the interpreting, and so on, and leap in to share our message. The usual result is something that resembles less a conversation and more a competition.

Importantly, you are responding—i.e., what you say is in direct reaction to what they have said. It is an answer, something that connects to their contribution and expands it, continues it, even contradicts it sometimes, but still speaks to it in some way. Have you ever talked to someone who patiently waited for you to stop, then proceeded to talk about something completely different? Chances are you not only felt they weren't listening, you probably felt invalidated or a little insulted, too. Good dialogues are co-created—they are not simply two people monologuing beside one another.

If during the course of the other person's speaking, you watch as your chance to share a particular idea has come and gone, do not try to force the conversation to backtrack so you can make your point. Let it go and engage with the conversation where it stands. When you "rewind" conversations this way, you are essentially telling the other person that all of their contribution beyond that point was unnecessary and unwanted—don't be surprised if they quickly lose interest after that!

Your response should *demonstrate* that you have gone through the HURIER acronym and have not only understood but processed what you've been told. Reflect on their message and show them what that idea looks like in your world after you've passed it over your own perspective and values. In a way, it's this final step that proves to the other person how thorough your listening has been. This is because you actively prove that you have taken on board what they've said and engaged with it.

Example: You mull over the whole encounter and everything your friend has said, and as a result of all that processing, you say, "Well, you've clearly got a lot on your plate right now! I have to admit that these days I'm a little allergic to overtime myself and haven't done the daily grind for a long time. I think I just want to live a little more slowly, you know? Do you think you'll cut back at some point? Or are you enjoying the hustle and bustle?" This is a thoughtful response that shows that you've heard, understood, and processed what you've been told, and you also share some of your own perspective. It isn't judgmental, but curious and collaborative.

You may choose to respond in a million different ways, depending on the message and what your goals are. You may ask questions, show empathy, do a chunking up/concluding statement to signal the end of the talk, or dive in deeper to show that you're interested in continuing. Be aware that expounding on your opinion is seldom something that others appreciate or ask for.

Social media platforms like YouTube encourage a kind of illusory conversation that is really just an isolated person talking into a screen, with no chance for the listener to respond or steer the conversation. Consequently, people today lack certain listening skills and may mistakenly think that a good conversation is one in which each person gets an opportunity to opine and make a little speech. They may unwittingly focus on how to accurately express themselves and forget to make space for the other person's expression. Using the HURIER acronym, however, reminds you of the relative importance of different components of a conversation. It is almost always a good idea to *start* with a thorough and attentive processing of the other person's message, and only *then* launch in with your own.

If you routinely fail to do any of this, you may find yourself earning a reputation as a conversational narcissist, which is what we'll explore in the next section.

Don't Be a Conversational Narcissist!

The term was first coined by sociologist Charles Derber in his 1979 book, *The Pursuit of Attention*, but sadly, conversational narcissists have existed for a long, long time. **A conversational narcissist is someone who has, basically, failed to understand the social, collaborative, and joint nature of conversation, and who uses the medium instead to *gain attention for themselves*.** Instead of using the chance to engage with another to learn and connect, such a person uses conversation as a way to bolster their own ego, to demand attention and recognition—in other words, they see others as audience members!

Now, don't just assume that this horrible affliction just happens to other people. As part of his research, Derber listened in on more than 1500 talks and had to sadly conclude that *most* were conversational narcissists, despite being well-intentioned. Being self-absorbed and trying to make everything about you, it seems, is actually pretty common. But it also means that you are missing out on opportunities to have more genuine, more informative, more satisfying conversations with people (not to mention coming across as a bore!).

Conversational narcissism can be understood as a kind of default that we all fall into when we fail to make efforts to truly listen. Sadly, conversational narcissism tends to reproduce itself—a big trigger for behaving this way is often the sense that we are not being listened to, because the other person is too busy with themselves to pay us attention. Yet, the more we try to make the conversation about *us*, the more the other person feels the same way and responds by trying to edge their way into the limelight. Ultimately connection is lost and the conversation becomes a battleground or dissolves entirely.

The first step is to fully own your part of the conversational contract. You cannot do anything about other people's behavior, but you can go a long way to model genuine listening and create a frame of respect and collaboration rather than self-absorption.

Reframe the Way You Understand the Purpose of Conversation

Why do people talk at all? Is it to prove how great they are, to show off, to elicit praise and flattery? Is it to show how much you know or have someone agree with you and confirm your views? While most of us want to say *no*, be on guard for when you might be speaking within this frame. Constantly remind yourself that the overarching purpose of any communication is to connect. A good conversation is not something you fight over with the other person to win, and it's not something you begrudgingly share with them, anxiously waiting for your turn so you can snatch attention back from them. Rather, it's like a dance you do together, something you *co-create*. If you find that your conversation partner is seeming to get in the way somehow, this is a sign you're doing something wrong! It should never be a competition.

Don't Jump Ahead

We have all had the experience of quietly thinking to ourselves what we plan to say the moment the person in front of us shuts up. Our eyes may even glaze over as we stop listening to them and instead think about the fantastic argument we're going to make once they're done with whatever it is they're blabbing on about . . .

It's a bad habit! As much as you can, try to stay present with what the person is saying. Don't rush ahead to try to imagine what they are going to say next, and likewise don't start thinking of your own response. Remember the HURIER model and tell yourself that you can respond after you've really listened, understood, and processed the message. Another good idea: remind yourself that you actually don't have to respond at all. It is not a requirement for you to weigh in or for you to hurry to get your equal share of airtime. Confident, secure speakers don't need to dominate the conversation, because they prioritize the flow and are enjoying the dialogue—who exactly is speaking is not so relevant.

Avoid Advice

As a general rule, never give unsolicited advice—and be careful even if it is solicited. Ask yourself, when was the last time you desperately wanted to hear what someone else thought you should do? It's not often, right? But you probably do find yourself wanting to be heard, respected, and empathized with on a fairly regular basis. Commit to offering the same thing to others.

The truth is that most people give advice because they like the way it makes them feel: wise and powerful. Most people dislike receiving unsolicited advice precisely because they can sense this unconscious motivation. Rather than getting enamored with your own vision of what the other person should do or what their situation means, become curious about how *they* see it, what *they* value, and what *they* are trying to accomplish. If you catch yourself wanting to say, "Well, I think you should . . ." try asking a question instead.

Stop Centering Yourself

When you are being a conversational narcissist, it is as though you are moving through the conversation with a certain thought hovering in your awareness: "What has this got to do with me? What can I get out of this? How can I make sure this road is leading back to me somehow?"

So they may say something about scuba diving, and you immediately think, "What has scuba diving got to do with me? I know—I did a scuba diving course when I was a teenager, and I have a pretty funny anecdote about a stingray. When they're done talking, I'm going to share my anecdote."

Or maybe they say that they've gained five pounds over Christmas and are feeling a little bad about themselves, and you immediately think, "Well, that's sad and all but what can I get out of it? I'm pretty good at stuff like this. I know all about nutrition and fitness. As soon as they stop talking, I'm going to share my brilliant diet advice and then they'll think I'm clever."

Granted, few people literally think in such selfish terms, but the effect of continually centering yourself is the same regardless. Instead of talking about the other person, or about the topic in general, you are constantly making the focus of the conversation *yourself*. This is tricky because everyone wants to talk about themselves to some degree . . . but do it too much and people will tire of you and find you difficult to connect with. Imagine your attention and focus is a beam of light. Constantly shine it away from you and onto the topic or the other person. The frame is not "what about me?" but "this idea is interesting, what's this?" or "hey, tell me more about you."

Watch Out for Passive Conversational Narcissism, too

Our description so far has been quite over the top, but you can dominate conversations in subtler, more passive ways. If someone keeps sharing something with you, but you fail to ask follow-up questions, it's like you're being a tossed a ball that you repeatedly let fall to the ground. The "game" never goes anywhere. Sometimes people signal their lack of interest in someone else by simply not giving any supportive responses, not asking any questions, or even not acknowledging that they've heard the message. This can be a conscious or unconscious way of controlling the conversation, since eventually the other person will just stop talking . . . and then you can jump in and have the limelight again!

What If *They're* the Conversational Narcissist?

Sadly, chances are they will be, at least some of the time. You might be wondering if it's worth going to the effort of asking questions, listening empathically, and de-centering yourself if the other person will only grab the opportunity to hog the conversation. This can be tricky to deal with. Always start by giving others the benefit of the doubt and ask them about themselves before sharing details about you. If they simply never ask, well, you can politely disengage and make sure you're not wasting more time than you strictly have to.

You never have to suffer in silence while being talked at, and you shouldn't feel bad for wanting to disengage from a boring, one-sided "conversation." Try as much as you're willing to gently steer them onto something else, but if they're not budging, cut your losses and bail! Sometimes people are having a selfish day, and sometimes they're just plain old selfish. Be polite but end it. Whatever you do, don't get embroiled in a fight for attention—you can never convince a conversational narcissist to care about you, and you can certainly never beat them at their own game.

Summary:

- One of the easiest ways to connect with another person is to just ask questions. The right questions help you gather more and better-quality information, build stronger connections with others, inspire trust and liking, learn, and help other people learn, too.
- Closed questions (those that have very short or one-word answers) can be used to confirm your understanding, make conclusions or summaries, or set the tone and scope of a more formal or structured conversation. However, they can kill a conversation and make it feel interrogatory.
- Open questions (any possible answer) allow you to probe for depth and can keep a conversation lively and open-ended. Use both in the "funnel question" technique, which probes for information down a narrowing path of increasing detail, starting broad and progressively becoming

more specific. Start with open questions, then drill down for more detail as you go, eventually reversing the funnel if necessary.

- Good listening is a collection of different skills: hearing, understanding, interpreting, and responding. The HURIER method asks us to Hear, Understand, Remember, Interpret, Evaluate, and Respond, in that order. Remember that listening is active and includes both verbal and nonverbal material.
- Avoid being a conversational narcissist, who is someone who uses conversation to gain attention for themselves, rather than connect with others, share, or learn. Reframe the way you understand the purpose of conversation and understand that it's not about you or your ego. Avoid giving advice, interrupting (or thinking about what you want to say), or centering yourself in the dialogue. Similarly, don't be afraid to disengage when you encounter a conversational narcissist.

Chapter 5: When It All Goes Wrong...

Effective Conflict Resolution

Conflict exists whether we like it or not. **It's inevitable that disagreements will arise whenever and wherever people have to deal with one another due to their inherent diversity of opinion, taste, and experience.** In certain cases, conflict can even be thought of as desirable, since it ultimately strengthens bonds, forces people to communicate better, and helps them collaborate in realistic ways. In this chapter, we'll look at ways to manage conversations that have gone bad, or navigate those that may prove challenging.

In an article published in the *Journal of Managerial Sciences* in 2009, Professor Abdul Ghaffar of Qurtuba University argued that conflict is necessary because it draws our attention to the most relevant issues, encourages participation, helps people recognize and benefit from their differences, and raises awareness of problems. It can help both parties clarify their desires, blind spots, and boundaries.

The Different Types of Conflict

Most of us just want to avoid conflict, but this prevents us from learning more about it and becoming better at handling it when it inevitably arises. Not all conflict is the same—take a look at some variants:

Affective Conflict
"Affective" here indicates that the conflict is heavily tinged with emotion. Think interpersonal clashes that are filled with high levels of rage, fear, sadness, guilt, and so on.

Substantive Conflict
This is when people (often a group) disagree about the task at hand or the goal they are jointly working toward, i.e., disagreement over what constitutes a fact or "reality." In professional settings, it can thoroughly undermine an organization's effectiveness.

Conflict of Interest
This occurs when there is tension in how limited resources are allocated between two

or more parties. Usually, each party agrees on the fundamentals of the situation, but they are in essence competing for the same resources and are therefore at odds.

Retributive Conflict
As the name suggests, this describes a conflict where one or both parties is engaged in punishing the other for some perceived crime—usually an instance of that party trying to punish them!

Conflict in Values
This is not a disagreement about facts (i.e., what is) but about principles, values, and beliefs (i.e., what could or ought to be).

Goal Conflict
This occurs when people cannot agree on a shared goal.

Displaced Conflict
This is a kind of secondary conflict; both parties may shift their hostilities onto a third, unrelated party, or focus on irrelevant issues and fight about those instead of the *real* problem.

Of course, people are endlessly creative in the ways they clash with one another, so any particular conflict can be a unique blend of a few of the above or change over time from one to another. Understanding the type of conflict you're dealing with is a great first step in resolving it. As we've already seen, getting an insight into the unmet emotional needs behind conflict (that is, relatedness, certainty, autonomy, fairness, and so on) can give us a way forward in addressing those needs and relieving conflict.

The Thomas Kilmann Model

Kenneth Thomas and Ralph Kilmann are the two researchers behind this method of conflict resolution. According to the model, people come into conflict simply because they have different ideas, values, motivations, or wants. The main way around this difference is to use plenty of both assertiveness and empathy. Broadly, however, the model outlines five conflict-resolution strategies: **competing, avoiding, accommodating, collaborating, and compromising.**

Each strategy is a quite different approach to navigating conflict. None is *right*—each has their own pros and cons, and the one that will work best is the one that most accommodates the unique facts of the circumstances. Empathy and assertiveness are present in all five models, but in varying degrees. You can imagine a matrix with empathy on one axis, and assertiveness on the other. Let's take a closer look.

1. **Competing**
On the matrix, this strategy is high assertiveness, low empathy.

This is the tactic of working out disagreements using aggression or competition, which can be thought of as low-key aggression. Whatever the degree, it's about working *against* the other person, not *with* them. The strategy is great when you genuinely are in a position of control or authority, and also when you don't necessarily have the time, money, or energy to solve the problem or be overly empathetic. This tactic can actually work (if "work" means bring some kind of resolution to the conflict), but obviously, it won't win you any friends and your competition may alienate people to the extent that they no longer want to "play" with you.

2. **Avoiding**
Characterized by low assertiveness and low empathy.

This position is basically attempting not to engage at all. You don't defend your own position or make your point, but you're also not making any special attempts to listen to the other person's concerns. Naturally, there's a time and place for this approach. If you know for certain that you have very little power in the situation, and that the other person is unlikely to budge or listen, then it makes sense to just walk away. The approach becomes a bad choice if the conflict is actually your responsibility or even your fault, and a response to it is expected. Not responding can come across as disrespectful or weak and may actually increase negative feelings and create a bigger conflict down the road.

3. **Accommodating**
The approach using low assertiveness but high empathy.

This is the peacekeeper's tactic. Such a person will try hard to work things out, make concessions, and find some harmony. They'll tend to go along with satisfying others' needs just to keep the peace and err on the side of not expressing their own needs. This way of doing things is a good strategy to take when you don't have much power and are highly invested in a harmonious outcome. If there is a genuine but tricky conflict in a relationship that is very valuable to you, being accommodating can work—so long as it doesn't go too far and you become a doormat.

4. Collaboration

Uses high assertiveness and high empathy.

The approach of working together on a problem. Here, you balance your own needs and desires with the other person's, and you value both equally. A typical technique is to try to find some common ground or a shared goal and work from there. This approach is a great one if both sides can genuinely say that they want to come to an agreement. The approach will waste time and muddy the waters, however, if one or both parties is not really interested in finding a way forward—collaboration takes *both* sides working together, not just one. If there is low trust or reason to believe that there cannot be a reasonable shared goal, this approach is not ideal.

5. Compromising

This last strategy can be seen as the middling approach, somewhere right in the middle of both assertiveness and empathy. Compromising means embracing difference and disagreement without letting it jeopardize the relationship. It's a balancing act and a way to get people who disagree to nevertheless get along. Typically, the solution is for each party to move ahead with a plan that suits them in some ways but not all. Certain rules can be put in place to protect you, but you are also required to be flexible enough to abide by the rules of others, even if you don't particularly like them. It's an approach that can really work since both parties will by definition leave with something they want.

VOMP

You might like to combine the above model with another framework introduced by Crosby Kerr Minno Consulting called VOMP. **It's a simple acronym that can help you pause, regulate your own emotional response, and plan to respond in a conscious, measured way.**

Here's what the VOMP acronym means:

Ventilation

In other words, let people "air" their side of the conflict. So much trouble and misunderstanding can be avoided if people speak up and speak honestly. Keeping secrets, mulling silently over resentments, or even outright lying about how you feel will only prolong the negative feelings. But this ventilation process is not the same as solving the problem, nor is it a chance to escalate negativity by throwing blame or accusation. It's not necessary to decide if you agree or not, or counter with objections or corrections—just listen. Simply share your side of the situation and give the other person a fair opportunity to share theirs.

Ownership

There are seldom any conflicts between adults where there is a bad guy and a good guy, with the bad guy shouldering one hundred percent of the blame. Try to take responsibility for your portion of the conflict and "own" your part of it. This takes humility initially, but if you can acknowledge it plainly and move on, you may find it's actually a relief to stop being defensive. What's more, it can invite the other person to "put down their weapons" and frankly take responsibility for their portion of the conflict, too.

It's important, however, that you don't take on *more* than your fair share. Granted, it's not always possible to neatly portion out blame, and you might be arguing precisely because you can't decide who's more to blame. But in this case, say something like, "I acknowledge my part in the problem" in a more general sense, and move on. Never knowingly take on more of the blame in an attempt to gain an upper hand—it's dishonest and usually backfires.

Moccasins

This refers to the old advice to "walk a mile in the other person's moccasins. Both sides need to actively try to understand the conflict from the other one's perspective. Again, this is not the same as acquiescence or agreement. It just means that you make efforts to notice what the other person is going through and how they see things (including your behavior).

Plan

Finally, you need a way forward. Conflicts need to *end* at some point. Once you have both shared your views, listened, taken ownership, and so on, it's time to collaboratively decide on how you'll move on. What will be different? How will you avoid the same problem in the future? What rules or new expectations are there? Any new goals, reassurances, or commitments? Whatever they are, they need to directly address what each person has shared in a realistic and practical way.

Now, while the above may seem great on a theoretical level, you can probably already tell that it may be difficult to apply in real-life situations, especially when tempers are flaring. One of the best things you can do when you notice that a conflict is occurring is to *get a little distance.* Pause and make space. This will allow you to downregulate those strong emotions—which as we've seen get in the way of more rational thought processes—and help you slow down and look carefully at what is happening. The conflict will still be there, but you will have a strategy for moving forward.

So, a general strategy for all conflicts is:

1. **Pause and step away** (if possible). Use the distance to become conscious of both sides' unmet needs, their concerns, and their goals. Process your feelings and take a moment to cool off.
2. **Decide on a strategy** using the Thomas Kilmann model. Think carefully about the degree of both empathy and assertiveness you'll need to best resolve the conflict. Don't forget to think about the other person's approach, not just yours.
3. **Consciously attempt a conflict-resolving conversation**, as we've explored in earlier chapters on "crucial conversations." Plan a time and place,

conduct yourself with civility and compassion, and do your best to come to a mutually satisfying resolution.

Uh Oh—We Talked and There's Still Conflict

Let's be honest. You can do everything "right" and still find yourself facing an unpleasant situation. Sometimes, the best thing you can do is to compassionately detach and try to move on as soon as possible. Not every situation has a comfortable resolution for every party, and not every problem has a solution. Sometimes, hurt feelings remain hurt, and relationships or connections are damaged or terminated.

Nevertheless, even though you may find yourself in a stalemate and unable to compromise much further, try to at least come to some sort of inner resolution with yourself. Ask honestly what you can learn for next time. You will get over the dispute a lot faster if you know deep down that you have allowed the negative experience to make you a better communicator going forward.

How to Master High-Stakes Discussions and Stabilize Intense Emotions

So far, we've looked at ways to take control of your conversational frame, to convince and persuade, to ask useful questions, and to use tact and deliberation as you conduct yourself in dialogue. All of this, however, becomes far more difficult if we find ourselves in the middle of a distressing conflict situation. Chances are, you've been there before: Emotions are running high, things feel a little volatile and unpleasant, and you may even notice that you're acting impulsively . . . sometimes to your later regret.

Conflict is human, and being destabilized now and then does not mean you are a poor communicator. Nevertheless, it is possible to learn skills that will help you navigate these tricky situations *as they are happening*—which is the time when you most need to communicate well!

Let's talk about **crucial conversations**. These kinds of talks combine three key features:

1. High stakes (i.e., there is a lot to lose on both sides)
2. Opposing viewpoints

3. Strong emotions

Notice that in the list above, we have not mentioned the topic of conversation—people can and do get into conflict over "minor" or "unimportant" topics. The truth is that the topic is usually secondary. What's primary is what is currently at risk, how both parties are differing in the way they are approaching that risk, and the (let's face it, interfering) effect of strong emotions like fear and anger.

Let's all own up to it now: Most of us are simply not very good at crucial conversations. If something is important to us and we sense threat, strong emotions result . . . and that usually sees calm rationality and control fly out the window. If the other person does the same, you have a spiral that carries you both down into conflict. Have you ever considered that every single act of *physical* aggression started out as a verbal disagreement, maybe even just a silly misunderstanding? In other words, the spiral can take you far, far away from where you want to be.

Returning to our metaphor of the ladder of inference, it's clear how different beliefs, experiences, emotions, and perspectives create our "pool of meaning" and potentially lead to us clashing with someone who has done the same thing, only with a very different set of raw ingredients. Many would argue that it's easy to be a good communicator when the stakes are low—everyone agrees and the feeling either way is pretty neutral. But you will really put your communication mastery to the test by seeing how well you can navigate, defuse, and resolve conflict as it unfolds in the moment.

Whether your crucial conversation is to give negative feedback, to break up with someone, to apologize for a wrongdoing, to ask an embarrassing question, to set a difficult boundary, to clear up a confusing misunderstanding, to find a compromise between two opposing needs and rights, to smooth over hurt feelings, to restore trust, to solve a shared problem, or to cut off contact entirely, know that everyone finds these kinds of conversations difficult. Also know that in a very tricky conversation, there is seldom a way through that is completely easy and painless. So, keep that in mind as you read about the ways you can ease a conflict. No matter what happens or how badly things have already deteriorated, you can still do your best to move forward with respect, dignity, and a spirit of cooperation.

How to Navigate a Crucial Conversation

First and foremost, be as clear as possible from the outset exactly what the problem is. What is the issue, concern, or conflict? It seems too obvious, but before you get engrossed talking to the other person, clarify in your own mind what you see as having gone wrong. Is it one event or a pattern? Try to locate the issue and be as concise as you can.

This will help you **understand the purpose for the conversation**. The purpose should be, naturally, to address the problem you've identified. If you simply bring a grievance or a boatload of unhappy feelings to place at the other person's feet, it will only be felt like an attack or a confrontation. Know *why* you are having this difficult discussion, i.e., what you hope to actually achieve when it's done. If we're honest with ourselves, we may be tempted to start a conversation for the unconscious reason of hurting the other person somehow.

Once you are clear on all this, you can plan ahead and **choose a time and place to have the discussion.** Don't spring it on the other person or just launch into it without enough time to prepare mentally (granted, this is not always possible, but if you can, try to slow things down so you are in control and not merely reacting). Make sure you have a moment where you won't be distracted or interrupted, and avoid times where you know you or the other person will be tense or busy with something else.

Try to make the environment as supportive as possible. It might be a push to remain "positive," but you can do a lot to keep things calm, safe, private, and comfortable. It's far easier to deal with any difficult feelings or ideas when you feel like you're in a supportive "shelter" in which dialogue can unfold.

Once the groundwork is laid, the next part is probably one of the most difficult things any of us will be called to do in life: **be genuinely compassionate**. You will naturally feel some inner resistance to the other person—that always happens if the stakes are high—but the good news is that you don't have to agree with the other person or fake your feelings or allow them to mistreat you. You only have to maintain an empathetic awareness of the fact that they are also finding the situation difficult, just like you. That's all.

So, that's how you lay the emotional groundwork and approach the conversational space with an intention to listen, to cooperate, to resolve. Never underestimate the power of holding this attitude—you might not say or do anything differently, but your stance will be perceived. The next thing to do is lay the theoretical groundwork, and this means to **carefully separate evidence from interpretation, fact from opinion**. Usually, this is exactly where the conflict itself lies—each of you believes you are in possession of a fact, when really you are both arguing over different interpretations of that same fact.

Carefully teasing out what is true and what is merely a perception of or response to the truth can often make up the bulk of a difficult conversation. On the other hand, you might discover that you are both actually operating from a slightly different set of equally true facts—uncovering the assumptions on both sides can do a lot to lessen the size of the dispute, lowering those strong emotions.

As you talk, try to remember to "**question the question**." What this means is to dig a little deeper than the face value challenges, concerns, questions, or issues that are raised. This will help you move past knee-jerk reactions and overly emotional defensiveness and see to the real causes beneath. Ask yourself (or them!) what someone is *really* communicating when they say what they say.

But don't stop there—examine your own statements and questions in the same way and see if you can use "clean communication" to say what you really think, feel, and want.

Finally, the key to managing difficult conversations is to **take responsibility for managing your emotions**. Yes, you probably want the other person to do it as well, but you cannot do this for them! Stay calm and in control, and the best you can hope for is that it inspires the same of the other person. You are not required to lie, to be fake or overly stiff, or to assign yourself the role of "emotions policeman"—simply acknowledge and express your emotions but without letting them dominate or steer the conversation.

Regulating Your Own Emotions

You might like to reframe "controlling" your emotions as "self-regulation." Being in control of yourself emotionally doesn't mean you suppress, repress, or judge your own authentic emotional experience. Rather, it means that you never, ever allow this perfectly understandably human reaction to *get on top of you*. In a difficult conversation, you *will* feel strong emotions. But your skill as a communicator is about you feeling these emotions and doing the right thing anyway.

In his book *Emotional Intelligence*, Daniel Goleman claims that emotional responses occur far, far quicker than rational ones. The part of our brain that controls our emotions, called the amygdala, is activated long before we start using the prefrontal cortex, which controls our analytical thinking. This is a survival mechanism that evolved to let us react quickly to danger. The downside, though, is that it means we're predisposed to first act with blind emotion, and with our rational, conscious minds trailing far behind. If we know that when we're in the heat of the moment, we can't think as well, then the way to think better is obvious: put a damper on our emotions.

Dr. David Rock created the SCARF model in 2008 to help his patients better understand emotional reactivity and how to manage it during difficult conversations. Rock claimed that we need to start with an understanding of where strong emotions come from in the first place. He believed that people always act so to gain access to rewards while avoiding threats. They do this in accordance with five potential human needs:

1. Our need for **Status** relative to other people and to feel important
2. Our need for **Certainty** and knowing the future is predictable and in our control
3. Our need for **Autonomy** and the ability to feel like we determine our lives
4. Our need for **Relatedness** to others and to feel like we belong socially
5. Our need for **Fairness** and justice

If one or more of these needs are not being met, a person might start to react emotionally, since it feels like a threat. In high-stakes conversations, then, **one of our main goals should be to lower this sense of emotional threat so that we can start to access our slower and more rational thinking process—and find our way out of the problem**.

Sounds reasonable, but how do you actually do that? The steps outlined above (setting practical and emotional groundwork, engaging your compassion, planning a time and place, etc.) are all going to help, but so will some of the following principles:

- Before you do anything, just observe. Note your own emotional responses that you're

bringing to the table and try to put a label on them.
- Next, try to observe the thought process, interpretations, and personal narratives that are set in motion by these emotions. Take an inventory of your opinions, your assumptions, your understanding of the purpose of the conversation, your interpretation of a shared event, and what you see as the ideal outcome.
- Think about what your thoughts and feelings are telling you about the need that is currently going unmet. Are you feeling that your autonomy is threatened? Are you scared about losing relatedness or feeling angry about an attack on your sense of fair play?
- Use your understanding of all these things to start to put a frame around the discussion. These are not just space and time limits, but personal boundaries. For example, you might decide that you want to have a mediator present or make it clear upfront what you are and are not willing to accept during the course of the conversation.

If you find that your emotions are getting the better of you, stop, take a deep breath, and consciously remind yourself of why that emotion is there. Try to address it and then refocus on what you've identified as your goal. Keep your eyes on a potential solution and don't be distracted by emotion. If you notice strong emotions in the other person, you can do something similar. Try to ask compassionate questions to get to the root of what they're feeling and why, and try to find a solution in which both of you have your needs addressed. It will feel so much easier to get a handle on strong feelings if both of you know a potential way forward and have a clear plan for what can be practically done about the problem.

Assertive Communication

John asks Lana if she wants to hang out. Lana isn't interested in the least, but she's also afraid of coming across as rude, so she agrees. The two go on a date, and just as it's about to end, John pushes to meet again; Lana feels the whole thing is getting pretty awkward by that point, but instead of saying she's not interested, she makes an excuse . . . and a plan for date two.

Fast forward a month and John and Lana are having an outright conflict. Lana is mad that she's been pestered by John, and John thinks it's awful that he's been strung along. What part of their communication was wrong? Well, all of it—the moment Lana failed to communicate her position assertively, she avoided temporary discomfort and replaced it with a much bigger problem later on. In an attempt to not hurt John's feelings, she ironically ends up *really* hurting them.

Most of us feel a little uncomfortable "asserting" ourselves now and then. The thing to remember is that **communicating your needs, limits, and perspective with firmness and clarity actually saves you from a lot of future discomfort and awkwardness.** In fact, it can help you avoid a world of conflict and misunderstanding.

With good reason, most of us have been socialized to acquiesce, to cooperate and find harmony in social situations (some of us have been socialized to do this quite a lot!). We may unconsciously hold the belief that to be polite, we have to say yes . . . which means that saying no means we're being impolite. But is that really true? Sometimes saying no is the kindest and most courteous way forward, and saying yes is the quickest route to negative feelings, misunderstanding, and even disagreement.

None of us have infinite resources and infinite time, and this means at some point, we all have to choose what we want to focus on and what we will have to pass up on. Furthermore, we will often encounter other people who have made different choices about their priorities and values than we have. This means that we have to say no to certain ideas, events, projects, commitments . . . but also to people.

Good communicators know that this isn't a problem and not something you have to apologize for. In fact, gracefully asserting your own limits and boundaries is a way to help you more smoothly navigate social relationships, remove stress and drama, and command respect from others. It is never a zero-sum game where your needs and wants are pitted against someone else's—communicating assertively still leaves plenty of room for *everyone's* needs to be met, without resentment, passive aggression, guilt, or shame.

It may seem counterintuitive, but having firm boundaries that are well communicated can actually bring you closer to others. The first step is to drop the assumption that assertiveness means being forceful, rude, dominating, or unkind. It means truly understanding that asserting yourself does not diminish anyone else.

If Lana had kindly but firmly said, "You're great, John, but to be honest I'm not interested," it may have been awkward for a short moment, but ultimately, there would have been more clarity, more respect, and more understanding between them.

What Makes Assertive Communicators Different

If you're someone who can recognize Lana and John's story in your own life, you may have trouble asserting yourself. You may be an intelligent, self-aware, and well-spoken conversationalist who is good at listening and uses plenty of "clean" communication. Yet if you are routinely failing to speak up for yourself, and saying yes when you mean no, chances are you're going to have more than your fair share of conflict.

Assertive communicators are **not** loud, pushy, or arrogant. They never bully others, and they also don't make hints or threats or use other passive-aggressive approaches. To really understand an assertive communicator, you need to see that their approach is one of *balance*: what is being balanced is their needs, rights, and limits, and their respect for everyone else's needs, rights, and limits. They are essentially saying: *I value and respect you. And I also value and respect myself.*

The *and* is important. An unassertive communicator will value and respect other people but not themselves, and an aggressive communicator will value only themselves and nobody else. The effective, assertive communicator understands that the magic happens somewhere in the middle.

Ten Essential Assertive Communication Habits

1. **They make direct, clear, friendly eye contact**. They are present in the moment and aware of themselves and others. There is an honesty and sincerity in their company.
2. They hold their bodies in ways that are neither too rigid and stiff, nor weak and overly yielding. They **stand tall but relaxed**. They don't slouch or cower, but neither do they have any force or tension in their gesture or posture.

3. **They use a tone of voice that is steady, calm, and in control**. It is one hundred percent unnecessary to raise your voice to assert yourself. In fact, violent or overly emotional language most often signals a loss of control and lack of security in one's own position.
4. They have facial expressions that are **open and receptive**.
5. **They pay attention to when and where** they assert themselves by raising issues at the right time and place so they are most likely to be well received.
6. **They never, ever resort to blame or accusation**. Especially never threaten (for example, "If you don't do this for me, I'm leaving you"). When we try to manipulate people this way, we are essentially only communicating our powerlessness. Asserting ourselves is about knowing who *we* are and what *we* want. We are stating our limits on our behavior, not making demands on someone else's behavior. If someone cannot respect a boundary, then we follow through; we do not use our boundaries and assertions to control others.
7. They have **crystal-clear expression**. There is no room for wishy-washiness here. Say "I'm afraid I can't do that for you"

rather than "Hmm, this is a little difficult. I'm not sure..."

8. They use **positive language**. Having limits is not the end of the world, and saying no to something doesn't make you wrong or bad. That means it's perfectly possible to say no while keeping things friendly and polite. Assertive communicators also know how to frame their statements in terms of what is being gained rather than what is being lost. For example, "Could you put your socks in the laundry hamper? Then we'll have a nice clean room" instead of "Could you stop leaving your socks everywhere and making the place look like a pigsty?"

9. **They avoid criticism**. Again, for example, phrases such as "I know I'm being silly about this, but could you please not say that word?" and "Do you not have manners?" are just plain criticisms rather than assertions (and yes, one can be critical of oneself!).

10. **Finally, they gracefully accept when they are told no**. One of the best ways you can communicate to others that you take personal boundaries seriously is to respect other people's—no ifs, ands, or buts.

Well, so much for the habits of assertive communication, but that still leaves us with the question of exactly *how* to say no, to set down limits, to turn people down, or to raise grievances. Let's take a look at five different types of assertion—each one best suited for a particular social situation. Bear in mind that each will be most effective when the above ten habits are firmly in place.

Type 1: Basic Assertion

This is essentially a clear, neutral statement of our goals, ideas, emotions, limits, requirements, or feelings. It is something we are saying about ourselves. It is not the same as "truth," but it is the same as "our truth," and we state it plainly and confidently. For this reason, it's important for this type of assertion to use "I" statements.

"I can't eat dairy, as I'm intolerant."

"I feel a little disappointed that the plans have been canceled."

"I think this is a bad idea."

"I need to leave at five if I want to make my appointment."

Basic assertions are best used in those low-stakes, everyday situations where you need to make others aware of your needs, limits, and perspectives. They help us make the tiny course corrections to daily life that mean we avoid bigger misunderstandings later. Just remember to keep things short and sweet and don't make your claim as though you are inviting opinions or asking for permission. If you can't eat dairy, just say so with as much clarity and simplicity as you would say "the sky is blue." If you launch into a five-minute speech about why you can't and how you're sorry for being inconvenient, you're going too far.

Type 2: Empathic Assertion

Sometimes, though, what you are asserting will impact another person—sometimes quite negatively. The fact that someone will be unhappy with us setting a boundary doesn't automatically mean we aren't entitled to that boundary or that we are doing something wrong. But what it does mean is that we are obliged to consider and acknowledge their feelings. This is where empathy comes in handy. Crucially, empathy doesn't mean we capitulate to unreasonable demands or apologize for having limits. It means we have limits *while still having empathy for the fact that others might not like it.*

Use this type of assertion when you know that the other person might not like what you're saying. Begin with your acknowledgment of their thoughts, feelings, and opinions; genuinely and kindly show empathy for their position, then reiterate your own with the same level of kindness. Here, you need to pay more attention to finding *balance*. Making a firm assertion should not mean you're rude, and simultaneously being kind should not mean you have to soften your assertion.

"I appreciate that it's not convenient for you, but I simply won't be available that day."
"I know this hasn't been easy for you, either, but that's my decision."

Type 3: Consequence Assertion

Let's ramp this up a little. The consequence assertion is for those times in life when you need to communicate an if/then quality to your assertions. You need to let other people know that there are consequences to their behaviors and exactly what those repercussions will be. This can be an extremely tricky thing to navigate since the wrong tone or choice of words can make it seem like you are trying to forcefully control or modify someone else's behavior, manipulate them, or make ultimatums.

It's worth thinking carefully through your message for some time before speaking up. Sort it out in your own mind first and be honest about whether you may in fact be trying to strong-arm the other person or use guilt, shame, or obligation to control them. You need to understand for yourself how *you* will behave in certain conditions—not try to set the other person's behavior for them. Often, tactics like this can backfire because the other person calls your bluff, quickly revealing that you are not in fact prepared to follow through with the consequences, and that your assertion was nothing more than a plot for control.

Before you make a consequence assertion, ask whether there are other options before escalating this way. Only resort to this kind of assertion when you feel boundaries have already been violated or ignored, and when you realistically feel that you can and will follow through with consequences. When you make the assertion, keep all the ten points from above in mind; the firmness of your assertion comes from your own conviction, *not* from how blunt you are or how loud you speak.

"If you keep speaking to me like that, I'm going to have to insist we go our separate ways."

"Unless you can produce the documents we've requested, I will need to raise an issue with the ombudsman."

Type 4: Discrepancy Assertion

Of course, people do make mistakes, and nobody is perfect. Sometimes, people step over the line or break a clearly stated boundary by accident or just because they're not paying attention. If you've already made an agreement with someone and they then fail to follow up on their side of the deal, then you may need to make a discrepancy assertion. This is when you draw the other person's attention to the difference between what was promised and what was delivered. In a way, agreements, contracts, and deals are simply boundaries that both parties set. If you're in a professional or more formal context, you will need to know how to politely but firmly draw attention to moments when agreements have been dishonored.

The best way to do this is to frame it initially as a misunderstanding, and position the request for correction as something that you are *jointly* embarking on:

"The requested documents appear to not have been submitted yet. If they already have, please ignore this message and accept our apologies. If not, please be reminded that the due date has now passed, which is in violation of the contract."

This frames the issue neutrally, without making threats or placing blame, but rather shining a light on a discrepancy and subtly pointing out the natural, obvious consequences. Should such an assertion *still* be ignored, then the clear next step is to follow through with those consequences.

Type 5: Negative Feelings Assertion

If you have a personal situation in which you have a strong grievance you want to share with the other person, then you need to know how to assert how you feel. You want to call attention to the negative feelings you're experiencing as a result of their behavior. This can be done in a calm, controlled, and, yes, even respectful way. You will feel better for articulating your pain, and you will also give the other person plenty of opportunity to rectify things.

Importantly, this is the kind of assertion best made in private, in interpersonal relationships, and is usually inappropriate for professional contexts. Include a few key components: an objective description of their behavior, the objective impact of that behavior on you, your feelings as a result, and a clear statement for how you wish them to behave in the future:

"You were half an hour late this morning. As a result, I missed my appointment and won't get another one for two weeks. I'm absolutely livid. I need you to promise me that this won't happen again, and that you'll set alarms for yourself like we talked about."

Bonus: The Broken Record Technique

In an ideal world, you'd state your boundary and people would instantly hear you and respect your limits. In the real world, there are some people who can't help but test this boundary and push and push to see how much you really mean it (for example, every two-year-old in the world!). Such boundary-pushers will try all sorts of tactics to get you to budge. The broken record technique, however, makes you impervious to these tactics, because you don't react—you simply restate your assertion over and over and over again, like a broken record.

If you budge even a little, the nagging might continue, so be sure to be boringly consistent and make the same assertion again till the other person gets tired of trying to push you. Though you can paraphrase the language, do not change the message in the least, or add or take away anything. Be like a smooth, grey rock that simply cannot be negotiated with.

"Can you look after Buster?"
"I'm allergic to cats. I can't, I'm sorry."
"But he'll be in the other room most of the time."
"I can't, I'm sorry. As I said, I'm allergic."
"But you won't even be spending that much time with him."
"Yeah, I know, but I can't. I'm allergic to cats."
"Wow, you are so mean, you know that?"
"Okay, fine, but I can't do it, as I said, because I'm allergic. Sorry."

Give and Take: The Art of Feedback

Effective communicators are just as good at giving feedback as they are at receiving it.

Let's take a look at each skill in turn. First, how do you *give* good feedback?

As with so many of the other communication skills we've explored, good feedback is done consciously and deliberately. Be mindful of your language and keep in mind the ultimate purpose of communication. In this case, the goal of giving feedback is not to shame, control others, or make yourself look smart. Rather, it's about communicating something that will ultimately be useful to the other person—and possibly to you as well. That means that your goal is to avoid as much as possible anything that will interfere with the other person hearing something genuinely useful.

The Best Way to Give Feedback

Whatever situation you find yourself in, try to make sure your feedback follows these criteria:

1. It is about actions, choices, words, and behaviors, and not about people

2. It contextualizes that behavior by clearly describing the effect it has on you

3. It is specific

4. It is timely (i.e., delivered as close to the behavior as possible while staying appropriate)

If you are unhappy with an employee's behavior, but you tell them while they are in the breakroom with their colleagues, "You're irresponsible and have ruined things with this client," then you have not given them feedback, but more or less insulted them. Notice that every one of the above four rules is broken. A better approach would be to call them aside in a specifically planned meeting and say, "Breaching the client's privacy by sharing their personal information is not only illegal, it reflects really badly on me and means I have a lot of work to do now." This is specific, delivered at an appropriate time and place, and targets what the employee has actually done, rather than who they are as a person ("irresponsible"). This passes the test of being "useful" because it shows the employee exactly what they have done wrong and why it has inconvenienced you, whereas the only response to the previous feedback is to feel bad!

Of course, not all feedback is this "negative." Sometimes you will want to let someone know when they've done something right, and all the same principles apply. Sure, sometimes you just want to compliment someone, but if you intend to give feedback, be specific and make sure it's something the other person can actually use or act on. For example, "You're such an amazing employee" may feel nice, but "I really appreciate how you take initiative—it makes my life so much easier!" is more actionable and useful.

The Situation-Behavior-Impact (SBI) model is a framework that can help you ensure you tick all the boxes when providing feedback. SBI makes it more likely that other people will hear your feedback and take it onboard, rather than resist it, ignore it, or take offense. Here's how it recommends you structure your feedback:

S is for Situation: First describe the situation. Yes, you guessed it—you should aim to be as neutral and objective as possible. Be straightforward and describe things how an uninvolved third party might describe them. For now, just state the facts.

B is for Behavior: Now you move on to describing the behavior of the other person. Again this is just description—you are not interpreting, passing judgment, or saying what you think either way. Also avoid trying to mindread and guess why they have behaved as they have, or what they want or value. You want to cultivate an open, curious, and respectful frame here.

I is for Impact: As before, state your own resulting thoughts, feelings, or behaviors. As far as possible, try to focus on information that is quantifiable or can be measured. Be too vague and you'll get lost. Instead, focus on external, observable behavior and describe it in terms of how you've experienced it. Importantly, don't make blanket statements about what their behavior *is* more generally. Stick to how it affects you.

If you follow the above outline, you will likely avoid a few pitfalls: you won't get distracted by irrelevant behavior or either of your personalities or values because you'll focus only on specific actions. You won't cause offense or resistance because you are not attacking the person but making observations about their behavior, and in such a way that they can't help but see the same thing. Finally, you avoid overstepping and making claims about their behavior more generally because you only focus on the zone of control you're in charge of: how their behavior affects you. In our previous example, if you had told your employee that their being irresponsible was something that everyone thought, and that they always behaved this way, and that they were probably irresponsible in their personal lives, too, you'd naturally be overstepping!

Instead, keep your focus narrow, stick to one issue at a time, and be specific with it. Try to avoid observations about their judgment, choices, values, personality, and so on, and focus on what they have concretely done. Rather than frame someone's performance on a presentation as them being nervous, focus on how they spoke too quickly or stared at the floor a little too much. And instead of saying something like, "People can't hear you in the back," say "I had trouble hearing everything you said."

Other ways to help feedback go down smoothly:

- Ask questions. Be curious about their perspective on the issue and show that you have respect for it.
- If possible, give the person a way forward: Make a plan for the next move. How can progress be measured? Let them know.
- Don't draw things out—receiving feedback can be uncomfortable, so get to the point fast.

The Best Way to Receive Feedback

First things first: receiving feedback (of any kind) is never a problem. Even if it feels really bad in the moment or catches you by surprise, and even if it seems dangerously closer to being an insult and doesn't follow any of the rules discussed in the last section. Being an effective communicator means you have enough faith in yourself that you do not fear other people's opinions, whatever they may be. That said, there will probably be times in life where feedback throws you. Here's how to handle it with grace and turn it to your advantage.

Feedback can vary according to two dimensions: It can be expected or unexpected, and it can be positive or negative. That gives us four possible combinations.

If feedback is expected and positive

Hooray for you!
This one's easy—celebrate your achievement and be proud of yourself. If you like, make a note of what worked and commit to continuing to do it.

If feedback is expected and negative

For example, you've been called in for a performance review after a disastrous year. It hurts to hear, but you know there's truth in it; the way forward is to take action. Set objectives and goals for yourself and get moving—don't allow yourself to wallow in self-pity or be tempted to passively blame others. One of the best ways to empower yourself in the face of shortcomings is to find out exactly what you can do to learn. Any temporary embarrassment you feel will fade away; in fact, you can take a less-than-ideal situation and impress others with your ability to turn it around.

If feedback is unexpected and positive

In other words, a pleasant surprise. Bear in mind that feedback isn't always necessarily correct—and that applies to praise and compliments, too. Think about how valid the feedback is and ask what you can do to apply it to your life if it is valid. What did you do that worked? Repeat this behavior or see if you can make it a habit. If someone has complimented a skill or attribute, see if you're doing everything you can to support and develop that trait in yourself.

If feedback is unexpected and negative

We saved the worst for last. Hearing from out of the blue that you've done a bad job can be difficult, and it will always be so, no matter how high your self-esteem! The first thing to remember is not to react immediately, if possible. Remember that strong negative emotions can dampen your slower, more rational mind from stepping in, so try to just absorb and process what you've heard before reacting.

Next, seek to validate what you've been told. Sometimes feedback is completely groundless; sometimes it's right on the money—chances are, your bad feedback falls somewhere in the middle. Be honest with yourself. Look at the impact you might have had on other people, and think about things you might have previously overlooked. Keep in mind that everyone will have different expectations, values, and beliefs. Keep in mind also that even if someone has delivered their feedback poorly, it doesn't mean there isn't potential value in what they're saying.

Once you've processed things in this way, again orient yourself toward action.

What can you practically change given this insight?
What can your next step be?
What new goals does this inspire?
What are you currently doing that isn't working?

Whatever you do, try to remember that **feedback is about actions, not people**. That means that even though it's human to respond emotionally to feedback, you can cut yourself some slack and resist judging yourself, your personality, etc. If it helps, reframe things so that there are always three parties: you, the other person, and the issue at hand. Whether you are giving or receiving feedback, try to imagine that you're always on the same side as the other person, and it's you versus the issue, rather than you versus them.

Summary:

- Conflict is inevitable whenever people differ, but it can be managed with grace and tact. Try to understand the type of conflict: affective, substantive, conflict of interest, retributive, conflict in values, goal conflict, or displaced conflict from somewhere else.
- According to the Thomas Kilmann model, people come into conflict simply because they have different ideas, values, motivations, or wants. There are five conflict-resolution strategies according to degree of empathy and assertiveness: competing, avoiding, accommodating, collaborating, and compromising. Each has pros and cons and is best used in specific

circumstances. Compromising (medium assertiveness and medium empathy) is usually a good bet all around.
- VOMP is an acronym that can help you pause, regulate your own emotional response, and plan to respond consciously during conflict. It stands for ventilation (speak your peace), ownership (own your part in the conflict), moccasins (have empathy), and plan.
- Crucial conversations are characterized by high stakes, opposing viewpoints, and strong emotions. Be clear and understand the conversation's purpose, then pick the right time and place. Show compassion, take responsibility, and separate fact from fiction.
- Regulate your own emotions by being aware of the underlying needs they express: status, certainty, autonomy, relatedness, and fairness.
- Be assertive and communicate your needs, limits, and perspective with clarity and kindness. Be clear, calm, firm, open, in control, and respectful. Decide on the type of assertion that best fits your needs: basic, empathic, consequence, discrepancy, or negative feelings assertion.
- When it comes to giving or receiving feedback, remember that it is about behaviors and actions and not about

people. Be kind, but also don't take things too personally.

Summary Guide

CHAPTER 1: COMMUNICATION FUNDAMENTALS

- Poor communication arises as a result of a mismatch of perspectives, approach, or conversational skill. People process information differently, but to avoid misunderstandings, communicate consciously and use the "ladder of inference." It shows the unique way that people use their experiences to make meaning: observations > selected data > meanings > assumptions > conclusions > beliefs > actions.
- Conflict can occur when people are on different rungs. To improve communication, see where people are and how their ladder of inference is working for them, then speak to that, in sequence, and without blame or shame.
- Good communicators deliberately create their own frames during conversations and position their line of thinking by using specially chosen words, expressions, and

images. Change frames and you change meaning.
- Deliberately engineer your conversational frame and invite the other person in using pre-existing concepts they're familiar with to improve the chances they'll be receptive. Remember that reality is fixed, but the *meaning* of reality is dynamic and subject to change.
- Chunking is about the way we group information. Chunking up is grouping specific instances into a larger overall abstract pattern or theory, while chunking down makes inferences from the general to the specific. Keeping the level of detail varied and appropriate creates a better flowing conversation than one that relies too heavily on chunking up or chunking down.
- It is a mistake to think that authenticity, expression, and sincerity are enough— *how* we articulate ourselves matters. Consciously filter what you say: Is it true, kind, and helpful?
- Take responsibility for what you say and practice clean communication—i.e., without hidden negative meanings.

CHAPTER 2: MASTERING STYLE AND TONE

- A few crutch words like *um, ah, well, you know, like, so, right*, and *okay* are natural, but too many can undermine your credibility and make it more difficult to understand you. Instead, become aware of the habit and consciously replace crutch words and empty language with confident silence. Being calm and thoughtful shows consideration for your audience and gets your point across more effectively.
- Likewise try to avoid hedging or softening language and instead be clear, concise, and confident in your expression.
- Your communication tone is like a vocal frame you set, so pay attention to whether you are being informative, humorous, respectful, formal, or informal. No tone is wrong, but a mismatch between tone and intention, or tone and context, can be a problem.
- Be especially conscious of upspeak (making statements with the intonation that belongs to questions), and ask whether it may be damaging your credibility or interfering with your message.

- With tone, strike a balance between friendly and business-like, confident and arrogant, concise and curt, emotional and merely compelling, and so on. Professionalism is about awareness and deliberately taking steps to speak in a way that gets you what you want while respecting the context and your audience.
- Especially with public speaking, use signposts—which are verbal and non-verbal markers that tell your listeners what kind of "journey" they're going on, where they are, and where you are taking them. Use a signpost every time you want to transition, give further detail, link points, change topics, offer a counterpoint, or summarize.

CHAPTER 3: PAINTING WITH WORDS

- If you want your listeners to really absorb what you say to them, paint them a mental picture. Do this by using vivid and concrete imagery, similes (using *like* or *as*), and metaphors to connect abstract ideas with more real-world ones. Use adjectives and interesting details and be a little unexpected.

- Language is musical by nature, and much of the meaning it conveys comes down to its rate, its articulation, its flow, and the way it moves through time. Pay attention to the rhythm and flow of your speech.
- In parallelism, we repeat certain structures to create an effect. Repetition drives our point home and makes it seem more true, as do alliteration (repetition of initial consonant sounds) and assonance (repetition of internal or vowel sounds).
- Human beings react not just to "information" but to narrative; to be a good storyteller, you need to go beyond sharing information and facts, and help your listeners form an emotional connection to what you're saying. Good stories enlist the use of our voice, body language, gestures, facial expressions, and even visual aids.
- Make sure that your story illustrates supports or connects to your larger point or circumstance. Set the scene but don't dawdle on unnecessary detail. Start with a bang and keep things at a moderate pace, being concise. Be relevant and interesting, and if you can, practice your story ahead of time!

CHAPTER 4: COMMUNICATION'S MOST UNDERRATED SKILL

- One of the easiest ways to connect with another person is to just ask questions. The right questions help you gather more and better-quality information, build stronger connections with others, inspire trust and liking, learn, and help other people learn, too.
- Closed questions (those that have very short or one-word answers) can be used to confirm your understanding, make conclusions or summaries, or set the tone and scope of a more formal or structured conversation. However, they can kill a conversation and make it feel interrogatory.
- Open questions (any possible answer) allow you to probe for depth and can keep a conversation lively and open-ended. Use both in the "funnel question" technique, which probes for information down a narrowing path of increasing detail, starting broad and progressively becoming more specific. Start with open questions, then drill down for more detail as you go, eventually reversing the funnel if necessary.

- Good listening is a collection of different skills: hearing, understanding, interpreting, and responding. The HURIER method asks us to Hear, Understand, Remember, Interpret, Evaluate, and Respond, in that order. Remember that listening is active and includes both verbal and nonverbal material.
- Avoid being a conversational narcissist, who is someone who uses conversation to gain attention for themselves, rather than connect with others, share, or learn. Reframe the way you understand the purpose of conversation and understand that it's not about you or your ego. Avoid giving advice, interrupting (or thinking about what you want to say), or centering yourself in the dialogue. Similarly, don't be afraid to disengage when you encounter a conversational narcissist.

CHAPTER 5: WHEN IT ALL GOES WRONG...

- Conflict is inevitable whenever people differ, but it can be managed with grace and tact. Try to understand the type of conflict: affective, substantive, conflict of interest, retributive, conflict in values, goal

conflict, or displaced conflict from somewhere else.
- According to the Thomas Kilmann model, people come into conflict simply because they have different ideas, values, motivations, or wants. There are five conflict-resolution strategies according to degree of empathy and assertiveness: competing, avoiding, accommodating, collaborating, and compromising. Each has pros and cons and is best used in specific circumstances. Compromising (medium assertiveness and medium empathy) is usually a good bet all around.
- VOMP is an acronym that can help you pause, regulate your own emotional response, and plan to respond consciously during conflict. It stands for ventilation (speak your peace), ownership (own your part in the conflict), moccasins (have empathy), and plan.
- Crucial conversations are characterized by high stakes, opposing viewpoints, and strong emotions. Be clear and understand the conversation's purpose, then pick the right time and place. Show compassion, take responsibility, and separate fact from fiction.
- Regulate your own emotions by being aware of the underlying needs they

express: status, certainty, autonomy, relatedness, and fairness.
- Be assertive and communicate your needs, limits, and perspective with clarity and kindness. Be clear, calm, firm, open, in control, and respectful. Decide on the type of assertion that best fits your needs: basic, empathic, consequence, discrepancy, or negative feelings assertion.
- When it comes to giving or receiving feedback, remember that it is about behaviors and actions and not about people. Be kind, but also don't take things too personally.

www.ingramcontent.com/pod-product-compliance
Lightning Source LLC
Chambersburg PA
CBHW020530080526
44583CB00013B/801